GLUTTONS
and
LIBERTINES

Human Problems of Being Natural

by MARSTON BATES

VINTAGE BOOKS
A Division of Random House, New York

This book is for *John* and *Fina*—
with no innuendos intended

CONTENTS

Gluttons and Libertines

1 ❧ On Being Human

Placed on this isthmus of a middle state,
A Being darkly wise, and rudely great:
With too much knowledge for the Sceptic side,
With too much weakness for the Stoic's pride,
He hangs between; in doubt to act, or rest;
In doubt to deem himself a God, or Beast;
In doubt his Mind or Body to prefer . . .

ALEXANDER POPE,
Essay on Man

EVERY SCHOOLDAY MORNING our son Glenn comes to the bedroom at a quarter to seven with cups of coffee. Nancy, obviously, has done a good job of raising our children—the oldest at home has the alarm clock, and they all take a certain amount of responsibility for keeping their parents in line. The coffee routine has now passed on through all four of them; and when Glenn goes away I don't know what we will do. Look after ourselves, I suppose.

I switch on the light and automatically look at my watch to check on Glenn's timing—we are all slaves of that damned clock. School, office, lecture, railway, dentist. They say it all started with the monastery bells of the Middle Ages; but however it got started, Time now permeates every aspect of our civilization. The slavery starts at an early age: the schools, whatever else they do, manage to instill an acute dread of being tardy in most children. A few rebellious people manage to be tardy for most of their lives, despite the pressures; but we hardly regard them as models of conduct.

Anyway, I try to make some bright crack as I check on Glenn's timing, but it usually falls flat because neither of us feels very chipper before dawn. I reach for a cigarette—a deplorable habit, but again I am a slave—and start the slow process of pulling myself together to face the world for another day.

I have been sleeping on a bed. This seems perfectly natural to me. But if we take "natural" to mean doing what most people do, it is rather odd behavior. My guess would be that perhaps a quarter of the people of the world sleep on beds. I suspect that the commonest sleeping arrangement is matting that can be rolled up and stowed during the day—which is certainly practical from the point of view of space utilization. In warm climates the most practical sleeping arrangement is the hammock—an invention of the American Indians. It is easily taken down if the space is needed; it is portable; it isolates the sleeper from creeping things on the ground; and it provides maximum ventilation. It takes getting used to; but so do most things.

The paraphernalia involved in Western sleeping become more peculiar when looked at in detail: springs, mattresses, sheets, blankets, pillows, pillowcases. Beds have a long history in the Graeco-Roman and Western worlds, but this total accumulation must be rather modern. Much of it I find puzzling. Our bed, for instance, has springs; but my wife has put a bedboard over them. Why not just have a board to start with? And then there are all of the rules for making up a bed, for covering it, for airing it. You could write a whole book about beds, and I suspect someone has.

Habitually I sleep naked. This seems to be rather aberrant behavior in our culture—or in most others. To be sure, I keep a dressing gown close at hand, just in case the house should catch on fire. But it appears that most men in the United States nowadays sleep either in pajamas (a word and custom of Hindu origin) or in underclothes (a particularly common habit with college students). A sociologist might study this, to see whether there is any relation between night clothing and geographical region, or median income, or level of education. I remember reading in the Kinsey report on the human male that nudity was an upper-class characteristic, which made me feel smug for a while.

Women, in my limited experience, cling to nightgowns, though they can sometimes be persuaded to take them off. Nightshirts for men became rare about a generation ago; I know a few people who still wear them—eccentrics, I suppose. It is curious how fashion penetrates even into the privacy of the bedroom. It may be, of course, that more women now wear pajamas than wear nightgowns—my figures on the subject are not really statistically significant.

I left myself smoking a cigarette and drinking a cup of coffee. I wish I could break that cigarette habit. Do you suppose anyone starts the morning in bed with a cigar or a pipe? It doesn't seem right, somehow. As for coffee— in England it would be tea—and mostly in the United States in a private home many people find it an absolute necessity to start the day with a cup of coffee.

Finally I get courage enough to crawl out from under the blanket into the world—or at least into the bathroom. Civilization does have advantages. I brush my teeth and exercise my gums just as my dentist has told me to—what a lot of trouble those teeth cause us! Then I shave. This is an ancient practice among some of the so-called "white" races which, along with the Australian blackfellows, are the only peoples with enough facial hair to bother with. It is said that the ancient Egyptians shaved off all body hair, but with us nowadays men limit the shaving process to the face. Our women shave their legs and their armpits, as I am reminded when I find my razor out of place. I cut myself, and I think that my wife will scold. She can't understand why, after some forty years of daily shaving, I haven't learned better. I don't understand either.

My morning routine has become quite fixed over the years: teeth, shave, shower. One summer at a conference I lived for a while in a dormitory and discovered that most of the people there took their baths either in the afternoon or evening. This came as a surprise—I had thought that taking a bath first thing in the morning was one of those basic laws of nature. I had realized, though, that men can be sharply divided into two groups: those that bathe before they shave and those that bathe after. The bath-first group believe that the preliminary soaping of the face helps soften the beard; the bath-afterward people (where I belong) find an economy of effort in using the shower to wash the shaving soap off their faces. But the subject of bath timing is apparently much more complicated than this.

Then I get dressed. What a long cultural history lies behind each action here! The males in our society wear "arctic type" fitted garments, an invention of the barbaric tribes of prehistoric northern Europe. Trousers, neatly preserved by the acid waters, have been dug up from Danish peat bogs. These trousers are convenient in cold weather, as any woman can tell you. The tropical draped garment, which carries over into the dress of our females, is more comfortable in hot weather. But comfort is a minor consideration in our clothing habits.

Each morning I have to face the problem of what to wear. I have lived much of my life in the tropics, and I hate the feeling of a tie around my neck and of leather shoes encasing my feet. But a professor is supposed to wear shoes, tie and coat. He is far less subject to convention than, say, a banker or a physician is; but there are limits if he doesn't want to be considered a crackpot. I want to play my role well enough to be accepted by the society in which I live, so most often (on days when I am due to lecture) I put on a tie and try to look respectable even though I feel like a fraud. My aim, as I phrase it to myself, is to be "a reasonable facsimile of a proper professor." But I don't know that I succeed very well.

Breakfast. "Glenn, you *must* finish your cereal." Eating soon after you get up is another of those fundamental laws of nature in the United States. In other parts of the world the fundamental laws of nature differ, but they are equally inexorable, whatever their form. Cereal, milk— whoever first had the idea of getting food by squeezing the udder of a cow or goat?—eggs, toast, fruit juice. In the South, grits come with the eggs automatically; at some line in Kentucky and Virginia these give way to hash-browned potatoes. To the west, grits disappear somewhere in Texas.

Thus in the matter of breakfast we have cultural diversity, geographical diversity, individual diversity. We conform with the common usage of our group in when we eat, what we eat, how we eat it. Sometimes, too, we diverge. I almost wrote "rebel" but such a strong word hardly seems appropriate for breakfast—though a child's reaction may be a real enough rebellion.

Quite unintentionally I have got into a curious situation in this breakfast matter. I have never been much given to eating, especially the first thing in the morning, and I solved the breakfast problem some years ago by the simple expedient of breaking two raw eggs into a glass of orange juice and drinking the mixture. The needed nutrients are present, with no time spent over the stove, no frying pan to clean—only a glass to rinse out. This seems to me eminently sensible. The rest of the household accepts my behavior, though no one has ever made any move to imitate.

For years I didn't have the courage to order this breakfast in a restaurant. Finally a friend who knew of my home habits persuaded me to try it: he pointed out that restaurants were supposed to serve people's needs, and why should I be afraid of what the waitress would think. This first try was in the French Quarter of New Orleans, and no eyebrows were raised. But when I gave the same order in cafés along the highway driving north, I met incredulity and reluctance. It turned out to be all right if I asked to have the eggs beaten in the juice—I suppose because everyone knows about eggnogs. I still haven't had the courage to order anything except an ordinary breakfast in the dining room of a proper hotel.

Such is the force of opinion governing human conduct even in a trivial detail. My conduct, at least. Then I stop and wonder whether I am peculiar. I suppose the average waitress in the average middle-class restaurant would definitely say "yes." On the waterfront they are used to the idea of raw eggs in beer, but they might think the orange juice odd. So whether I am peculiar or not depends on where I am, which opens up some large questions.

Everyone, really, is peculiar. Any biologist, used to studying the behavior of animals, becomes puzzled when he turns to man—and he is forced to the conclusion that the human animal as a species is peculiar. How did we get this way? And what does it mean?

We could say that human actions are never to be understood in purely biological terms. Like other animals, we have to eat—we need proteins, fats, carbohydrates, assorted vitamins and minerals. There is nothing unusual about these food requirements or about the way the human digestive system works. The process of metabolism with man, as with other animals, results in the accumulation of waste products which must be got rid of. The wastes take the form of urine and feces. The inner workings, then, are biological; but the outward actions, the modes of behavior, are something else again. Feces is just another word for shit—but see the problem?

I broke my leg a couple of years ago and learned many

things in the slow process of recovery. The hospital immobilized me in traction and I remember, on one of the
first mornings, that a nurse came in and asked "Have you
had a B.M. yet?"

I was puzzled for a moment because they had been doing all sorts of odd things to me, and then asked her wonderingly, "But why on earth would they give me a basal
metabolism?"

It turned out, of course, that B.M. meant "bowel movement." Somehow I had got through life without learning
that particular circumlocution and it struck me as very odd
—one of the many compromises with reality that have
developed in the nursing situation. Because of our animal
nature, we produce shit more or less regularly, but we dislike to admit this openly and we cannot talk about it with
any equanimity. We would much rather pretend there was
no such thing—stopping off in a "rest room" when the
need arises—but in a hospital situation we are forced to be
somewhat more direct.

Obviously I am skirting over a whole series of somewhat
different problems here. There is the problem of action,
of behavior; the problem of symbols, of words; the problem of relations between the sexes (I would have been able
to talk much more directly with a male orderly); the
problem of dealing with new situations (I eventually
learned to cope both with bedpans and with nursing vocabulary). Yet all of these are but aspects, really, of the general human problem of being natural.

What does it mean, to be "natural"? Maybe it is natural
for man to hide himself when excreting. Then maybe it
is natural not only to hide the fact in the bushes, but also to
gloss over the action with a deceptive kind of vocabulary.
In many parts of the world the idea of decent and indecent
actions is entangled with the use of decent and indecent words. One could argue that it is natural for man to
treat actions and words as equivalent—at least it seems to

be easy enough to start a fight by calling someone a bad name. If excretion, though unfortunately necessary, is naturally bad, one can see how the word for it naturally becomes bad too. But this still leaves puzzles.

"Natural" clearly means quite a number of different things, so that, when we start to talk about it, we can easily become lost in semantic problems. I checked the unabridged Oxford English Dictionary and found eighteen main definitions for "natural," each with a number of subheadings. For our present purposes, however, we can reduce these to three general ideas, which can be most readily distinguished in terms of their opposites. We can use "natural" as distinguished from "supernatural," "artificial" and "unnatural."

Natural and supernatural need concern us little. Our scientific civilization assumes that the world is orderly and not subject to capricious intervention and control by spirits. There are many cultures in which spirits are just as "real" as sharks or leopards—and a great deal more dangerous and more difficult to cope with. But in theory at least we treat the events of everyday life as the consequence of natural, rather than supernatural, forces.

Artificial is an easy word in some ways, more difficult in others. Essentially it means man-made. This is clear in the case of artifacts. An artificial rose is made from wax, glass, paper or what have you, in imitation of nature. Yet, if we stop to think about it, the "natural" rose growing in our garden is also man-made—the product of selection, hybridization and cultivation by man, and unlike anything that occurs in nature without human intervention. We recognize this rather vaguely when we talk about artificial hybrids or artificial selection, but we are, in general, reluctant to face the extent to which our environment has been altered by our own actions—the extent to which, in this sense, it is artificial.

If we use artificial to cover anything made or altered by

man, the word really loses much of its usefulness. There is nothing natural left in the environments that most of us live in. To escape from an artificial world we have to go to the north woods of Canada, the forests of the upper Amazon, or the southwestern deserts. So much for the environment. But there is nothing natural left in human behavior, either: it is all governed or modified in varying degree by culture, tradition, opinion. We can hardly talk about artificial manners, for instance, because all manners are artificial; there is no natural man.

There may be a gain in the use of artificial in this very broad sense because we begin to see the extent to which human actions are the consequence of the human condition. We begin to see the hazards of trying to determine what is natural for man by studying apes or monkeys or white rats.

But if everything about man is artificial, if nothing is natural, does this mean that all human actions are unnatural? Clearly not, because we have shifted to another meaning of natural. Unnatural carries the idea of abnormal, unusual, strange. This doesn't help much: you can get into as much trouble with normal and abnormal as with natural and unnatural. We are involved with the cultural context in which all people live: what is unusual for some may be commonplace for others. For us it is unnatural to eat worms; for the Chinese, unnatural to drink milk. Sometimes I am driven to think that calling anything unnatural merely means that the speaker does not approve of it.

All of which sheds little light on the human problem of being natural. In the case of supernatural, most of us have no alternative to being natural during life, whatever may happen afterward. The sorcerers and magicians in our midst may think they escape this kind of naturalness, but the rest of us have come to view their claims dubiously. In the case of artificial, there seems to be no escape from artificiality into naturalness. Only in the case of natural versus unnatural do we have an apparent choice—which boils down to the question of whether or not to act in accord with the usual, the normal, of our particular culture, our way of life. We are faced with the problem of conformity, about which we in the West at least have lately become self-conscious.

One could argue that natural behavior is that usual to, or conforming with, human nature—but for that one needs a fairly definite concept of human nature. The anthropologists, with their descriptions of cultural relativism, and the psychologists, with their emphasis on individual learning and experience, have shown us that this is not easy. One comes to sympathize with the existentialist position that there is no such thing as human nature, that each man makes himself.

But if it is difficult to determine human nature, one can at least discuss the human condition, most easily in physical terms. Man is a mammal and a primate, which immediately defines many characteristics. He cannot spend his whole life swimming, like a dolphin; nor browse on grass, like a cow; nor scramble up a tree trunk unaided, like a squirrel or like some of his monkey relatives. He has an upright posture, with appropriately modified feet, legs and trunk, which makes him unique among the primates. His hands and arms, not needed for walking, are free for other functions, thus allowing him to develop his great ability at manipulating things. There are limits though: I have often wished, in situations such as cocktail parties, that I had a prehensile tail so that I could manage my drink, my canapé and my cigarette at the same time. A spider monkey would have no trouble.

Man has binocular vision, which enables him to judge distance well; and he can discriminate form and color. Many animals, however, have keener vision. Man's hearing is moderately good, but his sense of smell is quite poor.

One could go on with such a list and describe the anatomical and physiological traits of the human animal with some accuracy, and in so doing one aspect of the human condition would be described. But how little this helps us in understanding ourselves! No matter how much care we devote to the study of the anatomy of the brain, we learn nothing about why "shit" is an indecent word for a necessary action; nothing about why men wear trousers and women skirts in our culture; nothing about food habits or sex habits. Anatomy and physiology tell us nothing about shame, pride or modesty.

Our problem turns on the mind rather than the body: but how do we dissect the mind? It doesn't help much to say that body and mind are not separate entities, but simply different aspects of the physical organism. Maybe we should shift terms and talk, not about mind, but about self-consciousness or awareness. But we are still bogged down in words. How our awareness compares with that of a chimpanzee, a monkey or a dog, we do not know. Certainly we can find comparable expressions of emotions in animals and men, as Charles Darwin showed long ago. Perhaps from this we can infer comparable emotions, but it is difficult to find out about this because we cannot carry on discussions with other animals.

Certainly it is difficult to separate human actions, emotions and attitudes from the human habit of talking. It would be interesting to know how all of this got started. Did those ape-men living in South Africa a half a million years ago "talk" in some way comparable with ours? Did they listen to the advice of a wise old chief, and did they try to be faithful to their mates? Had they developed special ideas about food, sex and excretion—in other words, did they have cultural taboos? Which I suppose is asking how human they were. Their brains were only a little larger than those of modern chimpanzees: a cranial capacity of 450–550 cc., compared with 350–450 for the chimp and with 1200–1500 for modern man. But it is hard to know what this means in terms of behavior.

These Australopithecines—as the South African ape-men are properly called—were at least human enough to commit murder. Raymond Dart, in his book *Adventures with the Missing Link,* remarks on the jaw of an adolescent "which had been bashed in by a formidable blow from the front and delivered with great accuracy just to the left of the point of the jaw." Nothing of this sort happens in the case of squabbles among apes and monkeys, though they may be mean enough to each other when cooped up together in a zoo.

We have here direct evidence of a kind of behavior on the part of our remote evolutionary ancestors, though with no clue as to the meaning of the behavior; but even this much is rare. For the most part we have only bones and tools made of materials likely to survive—which tell us nothing about sex habits, or even skin color or body hair. We have, in short, considerable evidence to help us in reconstructing the evolution of the human skeleton, but almost none to help us reconstruct the history of human behavior. Yet our striking peculiarities are in behavior, not in skeleton. We can get ideas about the possible background by watching living monkeys and apes; but man is so different that these inferences must be interpreted with great caution. For the most part we can only speculate about the history of human behavior, bolstering our speculations with whatever evidence we can find. This is no road to certainty; but speculation often is the impetus for scientific investigation, and it can be illuminating.

The outstanding peculiarity of man is the great control of custom, of culture, over behavior. This is obvious enough in the case of such things as food, sex and excretion, but it is far more pervasive. We can't even get out of breath "naturally." If we are late for an appointment we may tend to exaggerate our breathlessness to show how hard we were trying. On the other hand, people of my age try to suppress their panting, trying to hide the deterioration of age—or of too much smoking.

The effect of culture on behavior is not limited to actions; it influences all physiology in many ways. This shows up in the psychosomatic diseases—ulcers, dermatitis, asthma and a host of little-understood effects of "mind" on "body." This relationship is especially irritating when you know that a particular worry is causing a distressing physical effect like dermatitis—yet you can't escape the worry. Here is where psychotherapy or drugs, benign or otherwise, come in.

Then there is the curious human trait of blushing, whereby thoughts influence peripheral blood circulation. Here again we run into the perplexing problem of consciousness: you can't stop yourself from blushing by deciding not to. The possible origin and meaning of blushing fascinated Darwin, but neither he nor anyone else seems to have arrived at a satisfactory explanation of the phenomenon.

There is also the opposite and equally little understood process of influence of conscious thought on inner physiology, as in the exercises of Yoga. Apparently there is little a man can't do to his body if he puts his mind to it.

The human habit of hiding physiology brings up the corresponding habit of hiding anatomy. This of course depends on the development of clothing—a subject that fascinates me and that I want to explore in some detail later in this book. It would be interesting to know how the idea of covering parts of the body got started, but we shall probably never have direct evidence. It is quite likely that clothing started, not as protection against weather, nor as a consequence of a dawning sense of modesty, but rather as one aspect of the general human tendency to tamper with appearance. The list of things that different peoples do to their bodies is both curious and impressive: cutting

hair; chipping teeth; painting, tattooing and scarring
skin; deforming the infant skull or feet; circumcising
the penis; cutting or enlarging the clitoris; cutting holes
in ears or nose to hang things from; draping objects
around the neck or waist or arms or ankles. The motive
among Ubangi women for adorning themselves with
ridiculous lip plugs is no different from the motive of
Western women who use make-up and hair curlers—or
from that of men who endure haircuts, shaves and button-
down-collar shirts.

Clothing probably derives from the habit of hanging
things around the neck or waist, or perhaps from the habit
of painting or scarring the skin. The advantage of an extra and artificial skin in bad weather would then be a later
and accidental discovery. The concealing function of clothing is surely a secondary development and even in our
society it is difficult to decide whether modesty or display
is more important in the design of clothes: witness the
bikinis, and the street-corner boys with their tight jeans.

I have not been able to think of any animal except man
that ornaments itself by picking up additions for skin, fur
or feathers. There is no argument about man's being a
peculiar creature. But there is also no argument—among
biologists at least—about his being an animal. The animal heritage is clear enough in anatomy and physiology
—in the form of bones and muscles and guts; in the need
for breathing and eating and excreting and copulating.
But what of our heritage in behavior?

Human behavior has long formed the subject matter
of a series of special sciences: psychology, anthropology,
sociology, economics; probably history and political science
should be added to the list. I can claim no special training
in any of these subjects—though I once flunked a course
in sociology. I am a biologist, and my special field as a research scientist has been mosquitoes and the diseases they
transmit. But I am also a human being, and I have long

been interested in watching other people and in trying to gain some understanding of myself. Somewhere, early, I came to feel that the behavior of the peoples of the Western world gave them no patent on the right way of living —no monopoly on either the satisfactions or the miseries available to our species.

Thus both the peculiarities of man as a species and the diversity in his ways of life fascinate me. It seems to me that diversity in itself is good; that there is no single "right way" for all people. I hope the reasoning behind my plea for diversity, for tolerance—and for the concomitant inhibition of destruction, which is so often intolerance— will become clear as the book develops. The peculiarities of man and the diversity of his accepted customs show up in any aspect of his behavior that we stop to examine; but they seem clearest in relation to those two fundamental drives of all animals—food and sex.

development of human nature,
physiological

II ❧ Food and Sex

> Consider the moral, I pray,
>   Nor bring a young fellow to sorrow,
> Who loves this young lady today,
>   And loves that young lady tomorrow.
> You cannot eat breakfast all day,
>   Nor is it the act of a sinner,
> When breakfast is taken away,
>   To turn your attention to dinner;
> And it's not in the range of belief,
>   That you could hold him as a glutton,
> Who, when he is tired of beef,
>   Determines to tackle the mutton.
>
> W. S. GILBERT,
Trial by Jury

FOOD AND SEX are different—almost anyone can tell them apart. But they are curiously parallel in many ways and sometimes they blend. In a few species of insects and spiders, the female eats the male—after copulation, when he is no longer useful. And food exchange of some sort is a part of courtship behavior in many groups of animals. In human behavior the parallels are shown by a whole list of words that can pass back and forth between the contexts of food and sex: appetite, hunger, satiated, starved.

From the biological point of view, food (nutrition) serves for the maintenance and development of the individual; sex (reproduction) for the maintenance and development of the species or population. They are thus two behavioral systems that are universal for all animals and plants. It is difficult to think of other, similarly universal behavioral necessities: dispersal, perhaps, some means of getting about, of moving or spreading; and survival, some means of defense or protection (this will be discussed in more detail later). But these goals are not as neatly clear as are the goals of nutrition and reproduction.

A biological species is defined as a population of individuals that form, actually or potentially, an interbreeding aggregation, separated from other similar populations by barriers to breeding. The barriers may be of many different sorts: genetic, physiological, behavioral. Hybrids, crosses between species, sometimes occur in nature, but they are much more common under human care, where the ordinary barriers to sexual contact are broken. It is difficult, for instance, to imagine a Brown Bear and a Polar Bear getting involved with sex, even if a male of one happened to meet a female of the other on some Arctic shore. Yet they did cross in the Washington Zoo, producing fertile offspring. But queer things often happen with animals confined in zoos—it is an unnatural situation.

Mankind forms a single biological species because, as we all know, individuals from the most diverse subgroups of the total world population are perfectly capable of interbreeding and producing fertile offspring—and often do, even though not confined together in a zoo. Such breeding barriers as exist are geographical or social—not biological—and are often easily transcended: witness the people on the streets of Honolulu.

Sexual behavior, then, is the cement that holds the species population together. Food behavior, on the other hand, is the cement of the biological community. The biological community—a quite different concept from that of the social community—is most easily described in terms of food chains or food webs. A forest, a pond, a coral reef, any biological community, is composed of the green plants that store up energy from the sun, of the key-industry animals that live directly off the plants, of the secondary consumers that live off the key-industry animals, and so on to the molds and bacteria that reduce the animal and plant corpses to dust again. I like to make the quip that in studying the biological community, one is concerned with who eats whom; in studying the species, with who mates with whom; or, to use the ordinary Anglo-Saxon verb, who fucks whom.

Every individual animal thus must deal with sex in relation to its species or population, and with food in relation to its biotic community; and there must be satisfactory adjustments of both food and sex relations if the species is to survive. Man is an animal and in theory, at least, subject to biological laws, but culture comes in to confuse the biological regularities.

In general, throughout nature, sexual behavior can be studied in terms of reproduction. Mating occurs, for instance, only when the eggs of the female are ready for fertilization (or when sperm can be stored for future use), and there are elaborate mechanisms to insure the proper timing of events in the two sexes of a particular species. But in cultured man, reproduction seems to be an incidental or even accidental consequence of sex. Food behavior, similarly, can generally be studied in terms of nutrition, and food still serves man for nutrition just as sex still serves for reproduction. But it would be difficult to explain salad dressings, wine sauces or soufflés purely in terms of protein or vitamin needs.

It is a commonplace comment on Freudian psychology that its emphasis on sex comes from its basis in Western culture where sex is scarce—or at least strictly controlled —while food is reasonably abundant and generally available. The British anthropologist Audrey Richards, in rebellion against this preoccupation, set out some years ago to study human relations in an African tribe where sex was abundant and food restricted. In these circumstances she found, as expected, that food dominated the subconscious as well as the conscious life of the people. In her book *Hunger and Work in a Savage Tribe,* she maintains that food behavior in man is far more basically and extensively governed by cultural or traditional considerations than is sexual behavior, and she is probably right. Even in our own society food behavior is subject to all sorts of taboos and controls, though these have not been as thoroughly studied by psychologists and sociologists as have the sexual taboos. This is probably because we tend to find sex more fascinating than food—I suppose because we have more trouble with it.

I think one could safely say that there is no human society that deals rationally with the food in its environment; that eats according to the availability, edibility and nutritional value of the possible food materials within its reach. Very primitive, food-gathering cultures such as those of the Australian aborigines probably come closest, since they have to eat almost everything available and edible in order to survive. But even in such cultures we find special restrictions in regard to things like totem animals (those kinds used as emblems of, or thought to be the ancestors of, the tribes).

Our own food habits are certainly under strong cultural control, which has inconveniences even though it does not involve the conscious and subconscious frustrations of sexual controls. Some food peculiarities are shared by all Western peoples (the aversion to eating insects, for instance); some are national (like pasta); some are restricted to particular regional or social groups (like grits in the southern U.S.A.). None of us, however, can afford to look down our noses at other people because of their food habits.

I became conscious of this some years ago when I asked

a Hindu houseguest about his food requirements. He explained that he did not really have any deep religious convictions about food, but that he would rather not be expected to eat any meat from a cow. He said he supposed he felt about eating cows the way I would about eating dogs. I still have not eaten dog, but I think I have a better understanding of the Hindu problem from this explanation.

A dog taboo appears to be universal in Western civilization. A similar horse prejudice is more local to the United States, but still powerful. The Harvard Faculty Club started serving horse steaks during the Second World War, and as far as I know still serves them on certain days. My wife, trying a horse steak there, thought it was a fine idea and when she got home tried to buy horse meat from our butcher. But in our community horse meat cannot be bought through the regular channels; it is sold only as dog food. We made one experiment with the stuff sold as dog food, but it was not up to Harvard Faculty Club standards.

Even though repugnance to a particular food has a cultural rather than a physiological basis, the aversion can still cause a strong physiological reaction. The big lizards called iguanas are a highly prized food item in almost all parts of tropical America where they are found; the meat has a delicate, chicken-like flavor. But for some reason lizards are not eaten in Europe or the United States, perhaps because we do not have any suitable species: our lizards are for the most part too small to be of much use as food. But whatever the reason, we clearly regard lizards as unsuitable for eating. We once served iguana at a dinner party in South America. The subject had been thoroughly discussed, and we thought everyone understood what he was eating. Certainly all the guests ate with gusto. But as the conversation continued during the meal, a French lady who was present suddenly realized that the iguana she had been eating *était un lézard* and became violently nauseated, although a few minutes before she had considered the meat delicious.

I remember once, in the llanos of Colombia, sharing a dish of toasted ants at a remote farmhouse. This was my first voluntary experience with ants—I have eaten lots of them involuntarily, raw, when they just taste sour—and I found the toasted ants have a pleasant, nutty flavor. My host and I fell into conversation about the general question of what people eat or do not eat and I remarked that in my country people ate the legs of frogs. The very thought of this filled my ant-eating friends with horror; it was as though I had mentioned some repulsive sex habit.

Certainly what is repulsive and what is accepted and gratifying varies greatly among different peoples both with food and with sex. Look at the differing cultural attitudes toward kissing, for instance. The idea of putting mouth on mouth is unthinkable in Micronesia—and I often wonder what the Micronesians would think of the display near a girls' dormitory at an American university just before check-in time. For the Micronesians, as for many other peoples, the female breast has no sexual significance; it is an organ for providing food for the nursing infant. Yet among us, it has come to be highly erotic—look at the advertisements. We must seem very queer to non-breast-loving cultures.

The anthropologists have explained that the kinds of sexual behavior regarded as perverse vary greatly from culture to culture, but neither they nor the psychologists have bothered much about food perversions. Maybe we are surrounded by food perverts, undetected and unclassified, undermining the fiber of our civilization, infiltrating our diplomatic service, influencing our mass media, corrupting our youth. We need a Havelock Ellis to survey the field and a Kinsey to quantify it. Who knows how many people in this country put sugar in their salad dressings, make strawberry shortcake with sweet biscuit, use rice for dessert, or engage in similar abominable and unwholesome practices?

But I am being culture-bound. Rice pudding is not an offense against nature; it is merely a crime against the culture of people who believe that rice should be the basic starch of a meal rather than the dessert. If we tried to hold such cultural traits to be perverse, we would be faced with endless confusion. I suppose food behavior would be most truly perverse when it involved the intake of food for pleasure rather than nutrition, on the analogy that sexual perversion implies sexual activity unrelated to reproduction. The alleged custom of some ancient Romans of taking an emetic so that they could feast again on the tongues of larks would thus be a fine example of perversity. Chewing gum, someone suggested to me, could be looked upon as oral masturbation.

Dirt-eating, when it is related to a mineral deficiency in the ordinary diet, would not be perverse by this definition. But the use of the long list of substances that man takes for stimulation or hallucination or relaxation would represent perverse behavior. These substances may serve a greatly felt need, but the need can hardly be called nutritional. In many cases the substances are clearly antinutritional: the chronic alcoholic suffers, I am told, mostly from nutritional deficiencies.

It is curious how often these nonnutritional substances are taken by man—in other words, how generally people show perverted food behavior. I suppose it cannot be said that every culture has some drug to help its members escape from reality, but I would guess that the vast majority have, and of the most diverse sorts. Alcohol is the most widely used substance, and its virtues have been discovered independently by many different peoples, both in the New World and the Old. They have found a number of quite different ways of producing alcohol: through al-

lowing the sweet sap of palms and other plants to ferment
and through fermenting a considerable variety of grains
and fruits; most curiously, through chewing starchy tubers,
like the Brazilian Manihot, and fermenting the saliva-
mixed product. But alcohol is only one item on the list.
Primitive man must have ransacked the plant kingdom
to find substances that could be made into an alcoholic
drink, chewed or inhaled for a lift or for a temporary
escape into the world of dreams; civilized man still uses
drugs discovered by his preliterate ancestors.

These perverted food habits may be accepted and institutionalized by the culture, or they may be suppressed
or hidden or deplored—just as are the unreproductive
sexual customs. Our own culture is quite confused in the
matter, with every possible attitude represented somewhere. A few consistent extremists would suppress all
stimulants, even tea, chocolate, coffee and the like. They
regard them all as "unnatural." Tobacco and alcohol are
subjects of eternal debate, and many of us still have vivid
memories of our national experiment in the prohibition
of alcohol. Generally "drugs," from marijuana to heroin,
are strongly prohibited, though a vocal minority maintains
that prohibition is not the proper way to deal with the
problem of drug addiction.

We can call all of these things, by definition, perverse,
but that still leaves open the question of whether they are
good or bad. There seems to be no way of arriving at an
opinion outside of the cultural context. We could equate
"good" with "healthy," but we are still left with problems. All of these nonnutritional substances could probably be shown to be unhealthy in a physiological sense,
or at best harmless. But physiology isn't everything. The
Andean Indian apparently needs the lift from chewing
his coca leaves to help him get through the arduous days
of his bleak environment. I seem to need the lift of tobacco to get through my days, even though I am not ex-

posed to the physical discomfort of the Indian. How do we balance the physiological loss against the psychological gain?

There are similar problems in the evaluation of sex habits. If we define as perverse all sexual behavior not directed toward reproduction, we include masturbation, homosexuality, bestiality, voyeurism and the like; but then we must also necessarily include all contraceptive practices. Again there is an extreme but consistent view that regards all of these as bad ("unnatural") and another extreme that regards none as bad except where innocent individuals are hurt.

With respect to both sex and food it is clear that adult human behavior is largely a result of a conditioning or learning process. There must be basic, underlying drives for sex outlet—to use Kinsey's term—and for food intake, but it is hard to pare away the cultural overlay to show this biological basis. In the case of sex one can show a nice developmental sequence of the importance of learning in different groups. With rats and mice, learning seems to be of little importance in copulatory behavior—they manage quite well the first time. With animals like dogs and monkeys, learning is more important, and beginning sexual behavior may be awkward and unsuccessful. With the great apes, however, learning appears to be necessary for successful copulation. Individual chimpanzees raised in isolation at the Yerkes Laboratory in Florida had sexual urges all right, but no idea what to do about it when young adults of the two sexes were put together. Copulation is apparently always taught by an experienced mate. It seems likely, then, that this would also be true for man.

Food behavior probably also shows a similar sequence of the importance of learning, though I do not know of much good experimental evidence. I wonder whether, in man, there is left over an "instinctive" aversion to very bitter things, a reaction that would be of value in avoiding poisons. I think also of the dislike of some kinds of smells in association with food. But the dislike of nasty smells cannot be very basic in view of some of the cheeses that are prized, or the cult of high game; and then there is the famous durian fruit of tropical Asia, which is said to have a dreadful stench and yet to be delicious once past the nose.

Interesting individual and cultural differences are shown in whether particular foodstuffs are eaten raw or cooked, alive or dead. In general, only mute things are eaten alive—plants and invertebrates. If oysters shrieked as they were pried open, or squealed when jabbed with a fork, I doubt whether they would be eaten alive. But as it is, thoughtful people quite callously look for the muscular twitch as they drop lemon juice on a poor oyster, to be sure that it is alive before they eat it.

The moral problem of killing animals for food leads many people to vegetarianism. And where animals are killed for food, we have many laws to insure that the killing is humane—which means, I suppose, that squealing is reduced to a minimum. I think of the people of Samuel Butler's satire, *Erewhon*. The Erewhonians became vegetarian out of moral principles. But one of their great thinkers wrote a persuasive treatise on "The Rights of Vegetables" showing that vegetables, too, are alive and deserving of consideration. The Erewhonians, reduced to the logical end of eating only things such as cabbages certified to have died a natural death, abandoned the whole enterprise of vegetarianism.

There are numerous vegetarian subcultures, especially in Indian civilization and in our own, but voluntary avoidance of all meat seems to be limited to people at this sophisticated level of civilization. A goodly proportion of mankind lives largely on a vegetarian diet, but this is perforce because meat is scarce or too expensive. At the other extreme, Eskimos live exclusively on meat. Primates—monkeys and apes—are generally vegetarian or, at most,

eaters of insects and similar small prey. The adoption of
the carnivorous habit was probably one of the major steps
in human evolution, particularly because hunting, by
such a feeble creature as man, was linked with tool-using
and group cooperation, thus providing a base for man's
social evolution.

Vegetarianism now is frequently involved with religious
considerations of one kind or another, as food habits or
food restrictions often are. This offers another of the parallels between food and sex, since sex also becomes involved
with religion in the most diverse sorts of ways. There is a
basic difference between food and sex, in that an individual can refrain completely from sexual activity and still
live. Chastity can thus be a lifetime preoccupation, while
fasting is necessarily either of short duration or intermit-
tent.

I suspect that lifetime chastity, the cult of virginity, is
a trait of the sophisticated and complex cultures that we
call civilizations: it would hardly seem either possible or
worthwhile to cultures closer to nature. Yet such cultures
do have a variety of religious controls over sexual behavior.
Sex may be taboo before or during such special activities
as fishing, hunting or war. Sex may be required in relation to ceremonies to insure fertility of crops. Food or sex
may be involved in ideas of sacrifice, and the sacrifice may
require either abstention or indulgence. Thus we find
temple prostitution on the one hand and cults of chastity
on the other; ceremonies which require that no food be
eaten and others at which participants must eat.

In sophisticated situations, at least, one can understand
social and religious control over sexual and food behavior
in terms of man's efforts to master his appetites, and thus
to master himself. Neither the glutton nor the libertine
cuts a very admirable figure in terms of the moral or
esthetic values of most high cultures. Western civilization
in particular has kept the Greek ideal of moderation, of

temperance, though sometimes carrying temperance it-self to an unesthetic excess in the puritan and the prude.

In religious and social control of food and sex we are dealing with deliberate, in a sense voluntary, abstentions and indulgences. There may also be involuntary controls, perhaps more often with food than with sex. We find chronic undernourishment and malnutrition in many human situations simply because food is not available. And there has been, throughout history, a long succession of famines: epidemic, involuntary fasting on the part of large segments of mankind. It is more difficult to find examples of epidemic, involuntary chastity although, as a friend pointed out to me, this has occurred in certain situations like the gold rush to the western United States in the last century. The prostitution that builds up under such cir-cumstances is only a partial alleviation, comparable to the hoarding and black markets accompanying famines.

This makes one wonder about the saying that prosti-tution is the oldest profession. Maybe selling food came first. This is a meaningless speculation, of course, since both food and sex were commonly exchanged long before any idea of sale developed. From the accounts of the European explorers who first encountered the primitive peoples of the modern world, I judge that selling either fruits and vegetables or the services of women to the Euro-peans was performed with about equal alacrity or reluc-tance. Where the natives were reluctant, the civilized Europeans seem to have had little compunction about commandeering either the food or the women. It is odd, when you think of it, that we sell food openly nowadays, but in the United States, at least, try to prohibit or dis-guise the direct selling of sex. Some countries are less prej-udiced, and have just as opulent establishments for selling sex as they have for selling food.

Both food and sex may be given, as well as sold. Both are widely linked with hospitality: the welcomed stranger is offered something to eat and someone to sleep with. This can be embarrassing in both cases—if he is a fussy feeder and finds the proffered food repugnant, or if for cultural or esthetic reasons he is fussy about his women. Still, sharing a hard-won food supply or a treasured wife is surely the ultimate in the friendly gesture.

In general the question of who eats with whom and who sleeps with whom can become quite complicated, subject to all sorts of restrictions. The servants generally do not eat with the family, and we even have the phenomenon of exclusive dining rooms for corporate executives. We have nothing as elaborate as this for sex, perhaps because sex is secret with us, and eating open. If we had institutionalized orgies one wonders what would happen. As it is, there is a certain amount of protocol in sex, especially in the delicate question of who makes the first advance—whether in a marital or an extramarital affair.

But the etiquette of eating involves much more than who eats with whom: there are questions of what is eaten, how it is eaten, when it is eaten, what clothes are worn for the eating, whether talk is prohibited or required while eating. When one looks at all of the complications, it is a wonder that man has been able to feed himself at all; but it is also a wonder, in view of the complications, that he has been able to reproduce. Man seems to have got along fairly well on both counts—although it may be only in terms of a certain psychic cost.

I would like to explore the question of what is proper —what is "natural"—further in the case of both food and sex. Let's start with food.

III 🍎 *Three Square Meals*

Man ist was man isst.

(A person is what he eats.)

German proverb

B R E A K F A S T, lunch, dinner: surely the logical, the natural, way to eat, at least if you are a middle-class American. Three square meals, they are called, though in effete circles not much given to hard work, breakfast and lunch may be skimpy rather than square.

It might be more accurate to list the three square meals as breakfast, dinner and supper. Dinner, by definition, is the main meal of the day, whether eaten at noon, later in the afternoon, or in the evening. Through most of English and American history dinner has been a midday meal, only moving to the evening in fashionable English circles in the last century. The evening dinner hour still reveals both social and geographical variation. Dinner at eight is probably most proper, but Middle Westerners may eat as early as five thirty or six. In Mediterranean countries, on the other hand, hardly anyone turns up in fashionable restaurants before nine or ten.

Lunch, then, as a light meal eaten in the middle of the day, is a new idea. The earliest quotation in the Oxford English Dictionary is dated 1823, when both the word and the idea were still considered somewhat vulgar. Lunching thus may have been a habit among working people at an earlier time, without the word having appeared in the written language. The origin of the word is obscure, though dictionary people generally think it derives from "lump": a lump of bread or cheese. No one seems to know whether "lunch" is a shortening of "luncheon" or "luncheon" a genteel lengthening of the vulgar "lunch." The Oxford Dictionary people point out that it is possible that luncheon is an extension of lunch by analogy with punch, puncheon and trunch, truncheon. They find a 1652 quote on "noonings and intermealiary lunchings."

Luncheons may now characterize proper Bostonians and women's clubs, but lunches are common among working men and students, who carry sandwiches and a thermos of coffee or milk with them. Sandwiches, my dictionary notes, are "said to be named after John Montagu, fourth Earl of Sandwich (1718–1792), who once spent twenty-four hours at the gaming-table without other refreshment than some slices of cold beef placed between slices of toast." Some people consider this explanation wrong, maintaining that the inventor was the Duke of Shrewsbury and that sandwiches should really be called shrewsburies. The origin, in any case, was aristocratic and the first Oxford Dictionary quotation, dated 1762, refers to "twenty or thirty . . . of the first men in the kingdom . . . supping at little tables . . . upon a bit of cold meat or a Sandwich."

Nowadays sandwiches are plebeian, going to factory, office or school. I suppose the average person who carries sandwiches for lunch goes home to supper, even though this is now his principal meal: dinner has too elegant a sound. In England, of course, the workingman goes home to tea, which may be a considerable meal. "High tea" it is called, to distinguish it from the midafternoon affair.

This brings up the various small eatings that can be spread through the day. I like afternoon tea, and I wish the custom had penetrated the United States. Once, just back from Europe, I ordered tea in the club car of an

American train. I got it all right, along with appropriate pastries; but I still remember feeling very foolish sitting there with my tea while everyone else was drinking whiskey or something equally hardy. I abandoned tea for the rest of my trip.

In Latin American countries everyone stops in the middle of the morning to have coffee. This excellent custom has spread and in New York offices coffee now turns up regularly about eleven—almost as regularly as tea in London—and this is true in the American provinces too. In South America midmorning coffee often becomes a small meal, called *"onces"* (elevenses).

This seems to me ideal: breakfast, elevenses, lunch, tea, dinner, and a snack before going to bed. The three square meals have become six, and they have lost much of their squareness. I think one could argue that it is natural to eat more or less continuously but lightly: it keeps the digestive system working at a steady rate, instead of having it periodically overloaded. Some people, of course, eat continuously and heavily—but they are gluttons.

So much for when we eat. There is also a question of whom we should eat with. In widely different cultures, such as Western, Polynesian or Chinese, this turns on social status. We eat with people whom we recognize as social equals; or maybe we manage to climb; or maybe we condescend to share food with the lower orders. The relation between eating and status comes out beautifully in diplomatic protocol. I learned about this when I lived in Tirana, the capital of Albania, for four years, in the midst of a collection of diplomatic missions. Tirana may have been an obscure and minor post, but protocol was nonetheless rigidly maintained. Everyone knew his proper place at the dinner table, so he could go directly there without having to check all of the place cards. I had no status whatever, so I always headed for the middle of the table, remote from both host and hostess.

We lived in an old Turkish house with mud brick walls and a floor of mud hardened with ox blood. But we gave dinner parties too—very proper black-tie affairs. Once, bored with the fixity of protocol, we scrambled the place cards thoroughly so that no semblance of precedence was left. The dinner was not a success; everyone was obviously trying to figure out what scheme had been used in arranging the seating, and since there was no scheme, this was frustrating. At this dinner we had also made the mistake of asking ministers from two different powers. They spent the evening in a game of one-upmanship, without clear victory on either side. After that we stuck to the rules. Further, we adopted a policy of asking only one Excellency at a time so that he could sit at my wife's right and enjoy the nice warm feeling of being superior to everyone else.

In many areas of our rural South, and perhaps in other parts of the country, the women do not sit down to eat with the men, but serve them first. This, of course, is an example of keeping women in their proper place. The same end is achieved in the fashionable clubs of London and New York: women are not allowed to eat in the main dining room, or to come into the club through the front entrance. My wife has long rebelled at using the ladies' entrance or eating in the secondary dining room; as far as possible, she stays away from the clubs. What I don't understand is why the women don't retaliate by having a side entrance for men in their clubs. But club organization is an aspect not so much of food behavior as of the war between the sexes that smolders perennially in our culture.

There are many societies in which the sexes eat apart as well as many in which eating is segregated by rank. The rules for eating attained a particularly complex development in ancient Polynesia, in relation to the ideas of *mana* and *tabu*. Mana was a sort of spirit that infused people of great power or skill, was highly contagious and would damage lesser folk if they got infected. Since the mouth is an obviously easy way of entry into the body, particular precautions have to be taken against infection while eating. One could say that the tabus were the rules for avoiding infection—though I am oversimplifying of course. Great chiefs, because of their powerful and dangerous mana, became practically immobilized, lest they injure the people around them.

Some variant of the mana theory may explain many of the rules about who eats with whom in different societies. We ourselves still greatly respect the mouth as an entry into the body, reasoning nowadays from the germ theory of disease. When you ask what possible, dangerous germ could get on a spoon dropped on the floor, or migrate from the host's hands to the biscuit or the ice cubes, there is no answer. We are simply afraid of what might get into our mouths. I suppose it would be far-fetched though to explain the refusal of Southern restaurants to serve Negroes on the basis of fear of contagion with some Negro kind of spirit—particularly since it is usually Negroes who prepare the food.

Then there is the question of how we eat: of manners or etiquette and instrumentation. The manner of eating in any particular culture tends to be highly stereotyped— and to vary tremendously from culture to culture. It would be easy to say here that the "natural" way to eat is with the fingers; after all, they were made before forks. But eating with the fingers gracefully and successfully according to the etiquette of a finger-using culture is not easy; it involves as complex a learning process in high civilizations such as that of India as does the proper use of knife and fork or of chopsticks.

The present eating instrumentation of the Western world has been a slow development. Knives, forks and spoons each have a long history, but they did not come together on the dinner table until modern times. The fork was the last to arrive. A Byzantine princess brought a fork with her to Venice in the eleventh century, but this caused a considerable scandal and forks fade from history for several centuries. It was from Venice, however, that forks came into the modern world. Henry III of France discovered the use of forks there in the seventeenth century and introduced them to the French court. The first Queen Elizabeth of England is known to have owned three forks —two of them studded with jewels—but it is uncertain whether she ever used them instead of her fingers in the process of eating. The reluctance to adopt forks seems curious; the only explanation I can think of is the close association of forks with the devil.

The American colonists, like their European relatives, depended mostly on their knives and their fingers for eating; but the use of the knife for carrying food to the mouth seems to have lasted longer in the United States than elsewhere. Arthur Schlesinger Sr., in a book on the history of etiquette, *Learning How to Behave,* quotes the wife of a Harvard professor who, writing in 1836, insisted that "Americans have as good a right to their own fashions as the inhabitants of any other country." She defended the practice of eating with a knife "provided you do it neatly, and do not put in large mouthfuls, or close your lips tight over the blade."

The fork really came into its own in America after the Civil War: forks were designed for all sorts of improbable purposes. Schlesinger notes that a high priest of etiquette, writing in 1887, said that "the true devotee of Fashion does not dare to use a spoon except to stir his tea or to eat his soup with, and meekly eats his ice cream with a fork and pretends to like it." Americans are still fork conscious, with special fish forks, dessert forks, oyster forks and the like; and they place the forks properly to the left of the plate—but curiously they have never learned to use them with the left hand. British and Continentals are endlessly amused at the American habit of passing the fork back and forth from one hand to the other. I've spent a good deal of time trying to learn to pack vegetables expertly on the back of my fork, to avoid giving my English friends this particular source of amusement.

We can thus discuss at some length questions of when we eat, whom we eat with, how we eat; but the basic question, after all, is what do we eat. Here, as in so many other things, Americans are sure that they know what should be eaten. After all, we have the science of nutrition to give us the answers and every housewife knows about vitamins, calories, proteins and starch. I doubt whether any other people have ever been as diet-conscious as the contemporary Americans, or had such an abundance and variety of food. And I sometimes wonder whether any other people have ever eaten so badly.

The son of a South American friend came to stay with us a couple of years ago, while he was studying English. He was a big, husky, healthy-looking fellow—but he had deplorable food habits. He wouldn't eat his vegetables, nor would he drink milk. He preferred soda pop with his meals. My wife tried the system she used with our own children—they had to try one small bite of everything. Eduardo would dutifully take a tiny fragment of cabbage or spinach, but he never showed any desire to go further. He remained perfectly happy with meat, potatoes, rice and beans—for breakfast, lunch and dinner.

We figured he must be suffering from malnutrition, appearances to the contrary notwithstanding, so we made him take vitamin tablets—the nutritionists, with their fuss about balanced diets, have us well indoctrinated. Actually Eduardo did like fruit, and fruit was plentiful enough in his hometown, so I suppose that is why he didn't grow up with rickets or scurvy or some other horrendous deficiency disease.

Doubts about the dogmas of the experts on nutrition

creep in every once in a while. After all, the Eskimos got along very well for a long time on a purely meat diet; and their dietary troubles, it appears, have developed since the introduction of European foods. The famous arctic explorer Vilhjalmur Stefansson and two companions tried eating nothing but meat for a year; they conducted this experiment in New York under medical supervision. Even with the most elaborate tests no detrimental effects could be discovered.

Most of the vegetables that are so important in modern European and American menus are rather recent introductions. J. C. Drummon and Anne Wilbraham, in a careful survey of *The Englishman's Food* over the last five centuries, found little evidence of vegetable eating until the nineteenth century. The earliest surviving manuscript account of gardening, written about 1440, gave a list of seventy-eight plants suitable for cultivation, but almost all of these were herbs or simples. Onions, garlic and leeks were widely used, but the only other plants mentioned that we would call vegetables were radishes, spinach, cabbage and lettuce. It seems that vegetables, in medieval times, were more commonly eaten on the Continent than in England.

Fruits were plentiful in medieval England, but of course they were only available in the summer, and for a long time fruits were regarded with suspicion by most people, including physicians, as being liable to cause fevers. Much of the population then was probably on the verge of scurvy a good part of the time. Teeth though were in much better condition than ours.

Vegetables, to be sure, have a long history in the human diet. The Pythagoreans of classical Greece were vegetarians: they believed in the kinship of man and beast and in the transmigration of souls, and hence taught that animals should not be killed for food. The vegetarian philosophy of India also has an ancient history. Modern vegetarians are apt to argue that plant food is the "natural" diet of man because his closest animal relatives, the great apes, are largely vegetarian, as are most of the other primates. Unquestionably man can thrive on a purely vegetable diet —there are enough vegetarians around to prove this. And when such animal products as milk, cheese and eggs are included, the diet may be considered adequate by any nutritional standard. But as Stefansson and the Eskimos have shown, man can also exist on a purely animal diet.

I think that man is naturally a carnivorous animal, a predator on almost anything he can catch. It is true that other primates are largely vegetarian, but in many cases the plant diet is supplemented with insects, birds' eggs, or any available small animals. This is true, for instance, of chimpanzees, baboons, and of many of the monkeys. The great apes are more strictly vegetarian than most monkeys, but it is increasingly clear that human evolution and ape evolution have followed separate lines for a very long time, so that one must be cautious in comparing the behavior of present apes with that of ancestral humans.

Man's vegetable diet, without fire for cooking, is pretty much limited to special plant products like fruits and nuts. His digestive tract is simply not equipped to deal with cellulose and raw starch, which make up the bulk of vegetable material. The cellulose walls of plant cells are broken down by heat, and the starch is chemically changed into more digestible forms. Cooking, then, can be looked at as a sort of external, partial predigestion. Truly herbivorous animals always have some special way of dealing with cellulose: usually either some way of finely grinding the plant material with teeth or other mouthparts, or a symbiotic relation with microorganisms that carry out much of the work of digestion. Often both systems are present, as is the case with cattle, which have teeth adapted for grinding and flagellate bacteria in the first compartments of the stomach, where the breakdown of cellulose is started by a fermentation process. The human animal has no such equipment.

Man can, however, digest raw animal food without difficulty—anything from oysters and insects to fish and beef. In fact some nutritionists maintain that the digestibility of animal food is decreased by cooking. At any rate the evidence seems to indicate that the evolution of the human digestive tract, in the long period before the species acquired the use of fire, was in relation to a carnivorous rather than an herbivorous diet.

The evidence from archeology and paleontology supports this. One of the earliest hominid fossils yet to be discovered was found by L. S. B. Leakey and his wife in Tanganyika in 1959. They named their man Zinjanthropus. His remains were found along with crude pebble tools and with the bones of numerous small animals that apparently formed his diet. The inference is that this earliest man was a hunter, but not a very good one, unable to take on big game. Zinjanthropus is an early representative of the South African ape-men, the Australopithecines; and for these we have considerably more dietary evidence.

The Australopithecines were still pretty low-browed creatures, but they had made considerable progress in hunting skills. Raymond Dart studied 7,159 animal fragments left behind by a group living in a cave at a place called Makapansgat. He found that these represented the remains of at least 39 large bucks of kudu and roan antelope size; 126 medium-sized, wildebeest-type antelopes; 100 small gazelle-like animals; and 28 specimens of a tiny duiker-like species. In addition there were remains of 4 horses of extinct species, 6 chalicotheres (an extinct type of tree-browsing creature), 6 giraffes of extinct species, 5 rhinos, a hippopotamus, 20 wart hogs, and 45 baboons. Bones of porcupines, hares and water turtles were found along with this larger game. Fragments of eggshells show that the Australopithecines were addicted to bird-nesting, and crabshells show that they did not mind eating invertebrates.

There is no evidence that the Australopithecines had fire, and it seems most likely that they did not. But Pekin man, who may have lived two hundred thousand or so years later, clearly knew about cooking. The remains of some thirty eight individuals of this fossil hominid were found in the late 1920s and early 1930s in cave deposits at Choukoutien, near Pekin in China. Along with the hominid fossils were bones of a wide variety of animals, mostly of species that are now extinct—bison, horse, deer, camel, antelope and the like. The charring of these bones shows that Pekin man used fire.

How, one cannot but wonder, did our ancestors learn to maintain fire? There is evidence that grass fires started by lightning have a long geological history, far antedating man in many parts of the world. But a wildfire is a terrifying thing, sweeping all before it. How did any creature get the idea that fire could be controlled, maintained, used? No animal outside of the hominid line has.

Fire is spirit. Wildfire is a malevolent, destructive spirit, a powerful force of nature. Perhaps the first man to play with fire was boldly playing with the spirits. I can imagine some early human, venturing back into a burned area, daring to tinker with the tiny fires left behind, mere fragments of the spirit. He learned he could feed these infant fires and keep them going. He had caught a spirit! There would be no need for any practical use—think of the power and the glory of the man with a tame, personal fire. The fascination would be enough. We are still fascinated by fire, both as children and as adults. Even my dog will spend hours in front of the fireplace, staring at the flames, and I can share his absorption. Warmth, protection, cooking, all of the manifold uses of fire, could be discovered later.

It is often thought that the idea of cooking may have

started from tasting some animal that had been killed and burned by wildfire—reminiscent of Charles Lamb's well-known theory about the origin of roast pork. I wonder though whether there is any inherent preference for cooked meat in human taste. Most of us prefer cooked meat to raw, but we are taught this. An individual accustomed only to raw meat might well think that cooking spoiled the flavor. Innovation in food habits does not come easily for our species. I know that I find it difficult to eat well-done roast beef or steaks; I don't like the taste. I presume I got this attitude from my father, who also liked his meat underdone.

It seems to me perfectly possible, given the nature of the human species, that cooking got started for some quite irrational reason. The idea of fire as spirit, for instance, allows one to easily imagine the derivative idea that burning the meat with fire would infuse it with some of the spirit of fire—the eater in turn thus catching some of the spiritual qualities of the flame. Animal sacrifices are still often enough burned—and then eaten. A liking for the taste of roasted meat could then easily be a later development.

The beginning of the idea of cooking vegetable materials is another problem. Pre-fire man undoubtedly ate a variety of fruits, berries, nuts, shoots and tubers, and the idea of roasting or baking these may well have occurred quite early. Roasting would have greatly increased the edibility of many plant products, especially tubers. We still like roasted or baked potatoes; and other cultures get their basic starches from roasted breadfruit, taro, yams and the like. There is evidence from the excavations of the earliest villages in the Near East that wheat also was first parched, the roasted grains then being mixed with water to make a gruel. And recent studies indicate that the first use of maize, or Indian corn, may have been the popped kernels. Corn ears, in any event, are easily roasted.

Man could learn to roast vegetable materials as soon as he had learned to control fire; but he could not boil things until he had fireproof and watertight containers, pots—and this was very recent as we are reckoning time. Pottery was not invented until the time known to anthropologists as the Neolithic Revolution: a time of great improvement in toolmaking, of the beginning of agriculture and of settled village life. This revolution in human ways probably started in the Near East and in Southeast Asia some twelve thousand years ago—but Pekin man was already using fire several hundred thousand years earlier. With agriculture, and with pots for cooking the products, man's possible vegetable diet increased greatly.

I am always impressed and puzzled when I stop to think about the discoveries of prehistoric man. He must have explored his environment with great thoroughness, learning which plants could be eaten, which were poisonous, which served as drugs or medicines. We moderns, with all of our vaunted science and know-how, have added remarkably little to this environmental knowledge. We have, for instance, not domesticated any important animals or plants within historic times—at least no important new food source. The chief modern additions to the entourage of animals and plants associated with man have been laboratory animals like hamsters and fruit flies, or plants like the molds from which we extract penicillin. Even with laboratory animals, it sometimes seems to me, we have shown remarkably little imagination. Perhaps this is because with the development of civilization we have become ever more removed from the rest of the world of nature. In consequence we have been content to limit ourselves to the continued modification of the plants, animals and skills that were passed on to us by our prehistoric ancestors.

Primitive man, of course, had time. Given hundreds of thousands of years all sorts of things can be discovered by hit-and-miss methods, while the systematic investigations of science have only been available for a few hundred years. But even with an immensity of time, it is difficult to imagine how many of the drugs, narcotics and intoxicants were discovered, especially the substances that require rather elaborate preparation before they become useful. This is true also of some of the plant foods. The basic starch of the Indians of much of South America, for instance, comes from the tubers of a plant called cassava, or Manihot. But the tubers of the commonly used variety are poisonous, the juice containing hydrocyanic acid, so that careful preparation is necessary to make the tubers edible. How on earth did primitive man discover that a poisonous plant could be made into a food?

One can thus marvel at the knowledge and skills acquired by primitive man. But one can equally marvel at the misinformation accumulated in the course of cultural development; the superstitions, the taboos, the irrational actions, sometimes seem more impressive than the factual knowledge.

Superstitions about food involve animals more often than plants, probably because animals lend themselves more easily to animistic beliefs. Plants, for instance, are rarely used as totems. But there is plenty of meaningless folklore about plants. We don't have to leave our own society. I somehow acquired the belief as a child that it was dangerous to eat mangoes and drink milk at the same time; and I learned also that guava seeds and grape seeds could cause appendicitis. And for a long time our ancestors considered raw tomatoes to be poisonous.

Taboos on plant food are rather rare. Robert Graves cites one instance. He thinks that bean-eating was prohibited for men by the pre-Hellenic Greeks and that this taboo was carried into historic times by the Pythagoreans. Vegetarians and believers in transmigration, they apparently also thought that ancestral souls might reside in beans and the chance of rebirth be lost if the bean were eaten. This explanation is not very logical though because it was all right for women to eat beans. But then logic is not very noticeable in human reasoning about food.

Of course there are always explanations of food taboos, explanations that seem logical enough to the people concerned. The taboos and the explanations are particularly varied in the matter of what animals may or may not be eaten. The most rational people that I know, in relation to the food in their environment, are the Micronesians of the atoll of Ifaluk, where I spent several months. As far as I could see, they ate just about everything in their environment that was edible and considered tasty, including things that I did not think tasty, and things like sea anemones, that I hadn't known were edible. Yet they had two strong taboos: they did not eat shark and they did not eat moray eel. Their explanation, however, was at least plausible. The idea was that if they did not eat sharks and moray eels, sharks and moray eels would not eat them.

There is no evidence, as far as I know, that any of the animal food taboos are based on factual observation of ill effects. It is sometimes said that the Jewish and Moslem taboo on pork has a basis in the danger of infection by trichina. But this seems to be reasoning after the fact. It is much more likely that the taboo started as a reaction against a heathen pig cult which was once widespread in the Mediterranean region: only the worshippers of false gods ate pigs. Sometimes also it is argued that the avoidance of pork has a basis in the filthy, scavenging habits of pigs; but chickens have equally filthy food habits (from our point of view) and are eaten by peoples who reject pork.

Frederick Simoons has written a book on meat taboos in the Old World with the title *Eat Not This Flesh*. He points out that chickens and eggs are about as widely tabooed as pork, though by peoples who have been less well publicized than the pork avoiders. This taboo is particularly strong among many African tribes. Chickens most commonly are prohibited for women, but in some tribes they may be prohibited for everyone, or only for certain ages or social classes. They are frequently thought to be a cause of sterility, but a variety of other reasons may be given for the avoidance. Chickens and eggs often have religious significance, and chickens may first have been domesticated for purposes of divination rather than for eating. Most commonly prophecy depends on the angle at which bamboo splinters, inserted into the perforations of the thighbone, project. Cockfighting may also have sacred aspects, but cockfighting appears to be a trait of civilizations rather than of primitive tribes.

We are apt to feel superior to people who refuse on superstitious grounds to eat good food like chicken. But we have plenty of food taboos ourselves. One of the strongest of these is the taboo on eating dogs, though in many parts of the world dogs are raised for food, and in classical antiquity roasted puppies were considered a great delicacy.

The strength of the taboo is shown by an account given by Simoons in his book: "A good illustration is the recent case of Andrew O'Meara, a United States Army officer, who killed, skinned, and put a stray dog on a spit in Peoria, Illinois, to demonstrate means of military survival to some friends. He was prosecuted under an Illinois statute against cruelty to animals, pleaded guilty, and was fined the maximum $200 permitted by the statute. An interesting aspect of the case is that though Lieutenant O'Meara killed the dog with a sudden blow, and could have pleaded innocent, he felt public pressure sufficiently to plead guilty and to accept by agreement the maximum fine. The judge in the case had received crank letters and threatening phone calls, one from as far away as Washington, D.C., to make certain that he 'did his duty.' "

But in some ways the most curious of the food taboos of the Western world is that against eating insects. It may be interesting to explore insects as food in some detail.

IV ❧ Insects in the Diet

> . . . of these you may eat the following: the common locust in its several species, the devastating locust in its several species, the flying locust in its several species, and the grasshopper in its several species.
>
> LEVITICUS 11:22,
> in the translation of Theophile J. Meek

INSECTS ARE the most abundant class of animals on land. No one knows how many kinds there are because a large proportion of the inconspicuous tropical species have never been catalogued, but it is commonly estimated that there must be at least a million. And some of these, like houseflies in the Near East or mosquitoes in Alaska, occur in incredible numbers.

A great many insects are vegetarian, living directly off plants; when they in turn are eaten by other animals, the energy captured by the plants from sunlight is made available to the whole animal complex. Thus one can look at insects as the major "key-industry animals" of the land, to use a phrase coined by the British ecologist Charles Elton. Many insects, of course, prey on other insects or parasitize them; but all of these insects together form a basic food supply for spiders, fresh-water fishes, frogs and other amphibians, lizards and small snakes, and a wide variety of insect-eating birds and mammals.

Most primates are insect eaters. The few that do not deliberately hunt insects, like the howler monkeys of

tropical America, undoubtedly get many insects acciden-
tally along with their vegetable food—very likely thus
improving their diet. I have become most aware of
monkey-insect relations since getting a pair of marmosets
and a pair of squirrel monkeys (Saimiri), which I keep in
my greenhouse. Every day they are given crickets, bought
at a fish bait place. It is always a marvel to watch them eating these insects—they are like greedy children with a
supply of lollipops. I have never had the courage to see
how many one monkey could eat—I am afraid it would
make itself sick with a surfeit of crickets. And any fly that
gets into the monkey compartment is a goner; the squirrel
monkeys in particular are expert flycatchers. It is obvious
that insects are very good food for a wide variety of animals. But they are taboo for people in Western civilization. Perhaps this will change.

American food habits are changing. The popularity of
pizza is obvious enough proof, but there is better proof in
the great diversity of things offered for sale in any super-
market, or in the recipes included in any cookbook now
compared with one published a few years ago. The gour-
met may feel that we still have a long way to go, but
clearly we are moving.

In our household I am left in charge of one food department—things to eat with drinks. In the store where
I do most of the buying there is a wonderful assortment
of temptations: fish eggs of many kinds other than
the authentic but expensive caviar; fish of many species,
prepared in many different ways; a wide range of cheeses
and sausages, of crispy fried things, of olives and nuts and
minced clams and smoked oysters. Lately several kinds of
insects have appeared on the shelves: canned ants and silkworm pupae and bees from Japan, maguey worms from
Mexico, fried grasshoppers (the can doesn't say where they
are from). I have tried them all out on cocktail guests.
Mostly I must admit that they are not very good, but

this is not so much the fault of the insects as of the method of preparation. The Mexican maguey worms are almost as good from the can as they are fresh; and it is an interesting experience to watch a Midwestern housewife gingerly getting up courage to try a worm on a piece of toast —and then acknowledging that it tasted good, and trying another. .

It is difficult to understand our prejudice against eating insects. We are not against all invertebrates: we eat oysters, clams, snails, squid, octopus. Among the *Arthropoda*—the phylum to which insects belong—we eat lobsters, crabs and shrimp. True, not all of these are eaten by everyone, and some people will eat none of them. But they are rather generally accepted—in the United States snails, squid and octopus less than the other food mentioned.

It seems that we are reluctant to eat invertebrates that live on land, though it is puzzling why this should be so. Maybe the sea is remote enough from our everyday lives so that its inhabitants are unfamiliar as living creatures. In support of this we have the attitude of people in Florida toward eating land crabs. These crabs abound and they are, I know from experience, very tasty. But local people shudder when it is suggested, though the same people eat crabs from the sea readily enough. This attitude toward land crabs is a North American peculiarity. The Puerto Ricans prize their land crabs, and so do most tropical peoples. Our attitude toward snails also supports this land-sea theory: by and large, we have never really accepted these land-living mollusks in the way we have shellfish from the sea.

There is one striking exception to the Western refusal to eat insects—honey. To be sure, honey is not an insect, but it is an insect product—and a very intimate product at that, since the bees carry the nectar home in their crops to regurgitate it into the honeycomb.

Honey is an ancient human food. One of the famous paleolithic cave drawings clearly shows a man climbing down a cliff on a rope ladder to rob a nest of wild bees, a method of honey collecting still followed by the Vedda tribes of Ceylon. Bees, hives and honey are represented on the earliest Egyptian monuments, and the nectar and ambrosia of the Greek gods were both based on honey. The nectar of the gods was mead—a fermented mixture of honey and water which bee enthusiasts claim is the oldest of man's alcoholic drinks. Ambrosia, according to Robert Graves, was a fivefold mixture of oil, wine, honey, chopped cheese and meal. It doesn't sound very divine, but I haven't tried it.

In the Bible honey is coupled with locusts in several places. Honey is still on our dinner table, but the locusts are not, though they are eaten in many parts of the world, including the Near East. It is curious that we have acquired a negative attitude toward the eating of locusts and other grasshoppers. Perhaps it is because species of suitable size, taste and abundance are not available in Western Europe and eastern North America—fortunately for our farmers. Our grasshoppers are too small and too scattered to be easily collected as an important food item.

Even people of Orthodox Jewish faith in our culture are dubious about grasshoppers, though they are specifically permitted by the Jewish dietary laws, as shown by the quotation from Leviticus at the head of this chapter. There is some confusion in the Bible about the number of insect legs—Leviticus 11:21 in the King James Version reads: "Yet these may ye eat of every flying creeping thing that goeth upon all four, which have legs above their feet, to leap withal upon the earth." It is quite clear that the intention is to sanction six-legged grasshoppers. But all other flying, creeping things are an abomination, as are all things in the water that have neither fins nor scales.

Locusts are also specifically permitted for Muslims; it

is said that Mohammed's wives used to send him trays of
locusts as presents. There is some difference of opinion
about details, however. It is held in the name of Ahmed
that locusts ought not to be eaten if they have died of cold,
while the school of Malik holds that they are lawful only if
their heads are cut. But the majority opinion is that they
are lawful under all circumstances—though there is some
divergence of opinion among Muslim theologians about
whether locusts should be classified as land or sea animals.

There is no religious reason in the Christian tradition
for not eating locusts or grasshoppers. We learn from the
Gospel according to Matthew that John the Baptist,
preaching in the wilderness of Judea, "had his raiment of
camel's hair, and a leathern girdle about his loins; and
his meat was locusts and wild honey."

In the strict sense, "locust" is the word for the migra-
tory phase of a grasshopper, *Schistocerca gregaria,* that
abounds in the Near East and in north and tropical Africa.
The Greeks, fortunately for agriculture, did not have
locusts, but they did eat cicadas—quite different insects,
though they are sometimes called locusts in the United
States. Aristotle, in his *History of Animals,* noted that the
cicada nymphs taste best when they first come out of the
ground, just before the final shedding of the skin. But
he also found the adult males good—and the females even
better when, after copulation, they became swollen with
eggs. The high-pitched buzzing of the cicadas is a characteristic sound of the Grecian summer—a sacred sound.
Apparently Plutarch disapproved of eating them because
of this sacred character. He called the swallow "odious
and impious . . . because it . . . kills and devours especially cicadas, which are sacred and musical."

But to get back to grasshoppers: there are several
references among Greek historians and geographers to a
people called the *Acridophagi,* or grasshopper eaters.
These were small black people living in what is now Ethi-

opia. According to Diodorus of Sicily, they were short-lived because of the grasshopper diet, which caused all sorts of horrid things to breed in their flesh. Interestingly enough, there are actual cases in modern medical literature of grasshopper-eating Africans who became seriously ill because of intestinal obstruction from the indigestible legs and wings of locusts. This, however, is clearly a consequence of piggishness: the legs and wings are broken off by any civilized locust eater. A friend of mine, just back from Iraq, remarked upon the crunching sound made by squashing discarded locust legs as one walked across the room of a coffeehouse where people were having snacks with their drinks.

Wherever locusts and grasshoppers are common enough to make their collection worthwhile, they form a part of the diet of primitive peoples. They are especially important in many parts of Africa, and explorers of that continent have described a variety of ways in which they may be toasted, fried or boiled. Ground, dried and salted, they may be kept for months, making a food reserve. Grasshoppers were also an important element in the diet of some of the North American Indian tribes living in the Rocky Mountain area, where swarming species occurred.

Along with locusts and honey we might well consider the manna of the Bible as a possible insect product. Dr. F. S. Bodenheimer, professor of zoology at the Hebrew University in Jerusalem, wrote a book entitled *Insects as Human Food,* from which I have culled many facts. In this book he describes his efforts to identify the biblical manna. Some scholars have thought that it was a lichen, *Lecanora esculenta,* which grows on rocks in many parts of the Middle East, producing pea-sized fruiting bodies that are prized as sweet delicacies. These fruiting bodies are light enough to be blown about, so that they could conceivably form a manna rain. But it would be a unique event, and the Bible reports a regular appearance of the manna every morning. Furthermore, no one has ever found this lichen growing in the Sinai region.

There are, on the other hand, many reports from travelers in the Sinai region of a manna associated with the tamarisk thickets. This granular, sweet manna appears every year for a period of some weeks in June, though it varies greatly in abundance from year to year. It has generally been assumed to be a secretion of the tamarisk itself, but Dr. Bodenheimer, who visited Sinai to study the manna, found that it was the product of two species of scale insects living on the tamarisk shrubs. His argument that this insect is the source of the biblical manna is, for me, convincing.

Many kinds of insects that live by sucking the sap of plants produce sweet secretions. This is especially true of the aphids (plant lice) and scale insects. Ants have learned this and assiduously cultivate many species of aphids to get the sweets they produce.

The tamarisk manna is a rather special case of this general phenomenon. It corresponds in place with the biblical account: it is characteristic to this day of the parts of Sinai through which the Exodus passed. It corresponds also in season. The Israelites first discovered the manna on the fifteenth day of the second month after leaving Egypt, which Dr. Bodenheimer calculates would be about the middle or end of Sivan—late May or early June. Both the Book of Exodus and the Book of Numbers state that the manna fell at night. The scale insects produce their sweet secretion constantly, but it is most apt to accumulate in quantity during the night, when ants are not carrying it off. This is reflected in our own word "honeydew" and in the "dew of heaven" of other languages.

Moses required the Israelites to eat the manna on gathering it and not to "leave of it till the morning." Exodus 16:20 states: "Notwithstanding they hearkened not unto Moses; but some of them left of it until the morning, and it bred worms, and stank; and Moses was wroth with them." Dr. Bodenheimer notes that the "worms" could easily enough be explained as ants, which are very fond of honeydew and would swarm over it in an open tent. The "stinking" would, in this case, be a later misinterpretation and addition.

Dr. Bodenheimer finds many cases of manna production and utilization in the Middle East, although not generally noticed by European travelers. *Man,* he says, is the common Arabic word both for the aphids and for their honeydew; a *man-es-simma,* or manna from the skies, is often mentioned in Persian and Arabic pharmacopoeias. "We find that manna production," he writes, "is essentially a biological phenomenon of dry deserts and mountain steppes. The liquid honeydew secretion . . . speedily solidifies there by rapid evaporation. From remote times the resulting sticky, and often hard or granular, masses have been collected under the name of manna."

The *man-es-simma* of modern Arabic countries comes mostly from the oak forests of Kurdistan, and Dr. Bodenheimer considers that there is not the slightest doubt but that it is the secretion of an aphid, although the species has not been identified. The Iraqi authorities estimate that something like 60,000 pounds of this manna are sold annually in the markets of Baghdad and other places in the country. It is made into confections, mixed with eggs, almonds, and various essences.

The peasants of Kurdistan, who collect the manna from the oak forests in the coldest hours of early morning, believe that it drops from the sky. The manna accumulation depends on favorable weather conditions—no rain and cool winds. The gummy secretion of the innumerable aphids then drops and sticks to the leaves, branches and soil. Manna-bearing branches are gathered and beaten until the manna drops off; the crystallized substance, mixed with leaf fragments and dirt, is then brought into market and sold to the confectioners. Dr. Bodenheimer had a chemical analysis of the manna made and found that it consisted mostly of a rare disaccharide sugar called trehalose. He reported that confections made out of this manna were "delightful."

The sweet secretions of aphids, scale insects and the like are occasionally collected in other parts of the world where species with suitable habits occur, but they are always a rare article of diet, a special delicacy.

After honey and locusts, ants and termites ("white ants") are probably the most common and important insect elements in human diets around the world. Termites and ants are quite different groups of insects, but it is useful to deal with them together because of their parallel habits. Both are social insects, sometimes forming huge colonies of hundreds of thousands of individuals. Both show "swarming" behavior in that, at certain times of year, the winged sexual forms of a particular species will appear in immense numbers, boiling out of all of the nests in the region at the same time—a ready and tempting food supply for bird, beast or man.

Termites are especially prominent in the diet of many of the peoples of tropical Africa. Travelers, from the time of the early European contacts, have commented on this food, so that there is a considerable literature describing the various ways of collecting and preparing the insects.

Many of the African termites (as well as those of other parts of the tropical world) form large mounds that make striking features of the landscape. These mounds are often staked out as the private property of individuals or groups, and they may be valuable enough to be the cause of fights. Various sorts of ingenious traps have been devised to catch the winged sexual forms when they swarm out of the nests at certain seasons. Generally it is these sexual forms that are eaten, but some tribes eat the workers and soldiers, which can be obtained by breaking into the termite mounds. The big, fat termite queens, which may be two inches or so long, are always considered a great delicacy. But they live in special chambers in the depths of the mound, where they carry on their unending function of laying an egg every few seconds, and they can only be obtained by destroying the colony.

The Europeans who have been able to bring themselves to try eating termites have generally reported them as pleasant, or at least unobjectionable. The Africans have a more positive appreciation of the taste of termites. David Livingstone nowhere admits to eating them himself, but he does report on African opinion: "The Bayeiye chief Palani, visiting us while eating, I gave him a piece of bread and preserved apricots; and as he seemed to relish it much, I asked him if he had any food equal to that in his country. 'Ah,' he said, 'did you ever taste white ants?' As I never had, he replied, 'Well, if you had, you could never have desired to eat anything better.' "

Dr. Bodenheimer, with his usual thoroughness, has combed the literature for information on the nutritive value of insects. The results are rather meager, because Western dietitians tend to ignore insects in their nutrition studies. French and Belgian colonial agencies, however, have given some attention to the subject, and it is interesting that termites turn out to be among the richest of all foods in terms of calories, comparable with peanut oil. A Belgian analysis gave a value of 561 calories for 100 grams—several times the caloric value of local beef or fish. Apparently no study has been made of the vitamin content of termites; grasshoppers are rather rich in vitamins B_1 and B_2, and silkworm pupae in vitamin A.

Ordinary ants (as distinguished from white ants or termites) are also eaten in many parts of the world. The nests may be dug out for larvae, pupae and workers; but most commonly, as with termites, the winged sexual forms are eaten at the times when they swarm. In the small town in South America where I used to live, bags of the toasted sexual forms of the leaf-cutting ants were sold at the movie theater at the proper season. They had about the same quality and served the same function as popcorn. The Japanese now export canned fried ants, but these canned ants seem to me quite tasteless, lacking the crisp, toasted character that I remember for the South American species.

In the semiarid regions of the southwestern United States and Mexico, and in Australia, there are a number of species of honey ants. Among these ants, some of the workers convert themselves into living bottles, clinging to the roof of the nest cavity and taking honey from the active workers until their abdomens are completely distended. They thus form a system of food storage to tide the colony through adverse seasons. The Indians of America and the aborigines of Australia discovered this source of honey and utilized it as fully as they could.

The honey ants were especially important in the meager diet of the aboriginal Australians and were sometimes tribal totems. The Australian tribes, in fact, often had insect totems, which shows the importance of insects in their way of life. I have been especially intrigued by the "witchetty grub" people since I first came across them in the writings of Sir Baldwin Spencer, the great authority on aboriginal Australian customs. These insect-descended people, with their ceremonies to insure that their totem grubs will flourish and multiply, should have the sympathy of every entomologist.

Unfortunately no one is quite sure what animal the witchetty grub is—the field studies have been made by anthropologists rather than entomologists. Probably "witchetty" is a collective word for the larvae of several of the giant ghost moths that are as characteristic among the insects of Australia as are kangaroos among the mammals. Large, woodboring grubs are fancied in many parts of the world, even though they do not play as important a part in the human diet as they do in Australia. Generally they are occasional delicacies.

Among such delicacies in America is the famous maguey worm of the highlands of Mexico. This is the larva of a butterfly, *Aegiale hesperialis,* which bores into the maguey, or agave plant—the source of pulque, the national drink of Mexico. The same plant thus supplies the drink and the snack to eat with the drink, and the two have been combined by Mexicans since ancient times.

The maguey worms have been canned for the local market in Mexico for some time, and now some of the stores that specialize in fancy foods are importing them into the United States, as I remarked earlier. The canned worms are best if eaten hot; they have a pleasant, nutty flavor, which blends as well with a martini as it does with mescal, the potent drink that the Mexicans distill from fermented pulque. Maybe insects will get into our diet by way of this worm, at least for the cocktail hour.

So far, however, all efforts to persuade modern Europeans or Americans to eat insects have failed. There are, to be sure, traces of insect-eating in scattered places in Europe. Dr. Bodenheimer, combing the literature, has come up with a number of instances. It is said that the beggars of Spain and Portugal have the habit, widespread among primitive peoples and monkeys, of eating their lice. It is also said that peasants in parts of southern Russia to this day eat locusts, smoked or salted. The habit of eating larvae and adults of cockchafer beetles was probably once widespread in Europe, and there are reports of the custom surviving here and there.

Among Western peoples there are also accounts of occasional individuals addicted to insect- or spider-eating— usually reported circumspectly, as though one were dealing with a sort of sporadic and rare, but repulsive, food perversion. Gilbert White, in his classic *Natural History of*

Selborne, tells of a village idiot who, from childhood on, loved to eat honeybees, bumblebees and wasps, skillfully avoiding being stung. Dr. Bodenheimer finds mention of a young Swede addicted to eating ants; a German who spread spiders on his bread instead of butter; and of a young French lady who, "when she walked in her grounds, never saw a spider which she did not catch and eat on the spot."

In 1885 an Englishman, V. M. Holt, published a small book, now extremely rare, entitled *Why Not Eat Insects,* with this motto: "The insects eat up every blessed green thing that do grow and us farmers starve. Well, eat them and grow fat!" Holt was fully aware of the anti-insect prejudice, but he pointed out that many people freely eat cheese mites as part of the cheese; why not eat cabbage worms as part of the cabbage? After a review of insect-eating in classical times and among primitive peoples, he gave a series of recipes which he had worked out and tested. A sample menu will give the idea:

Snail Soup

Fried Soles with Woodlouse Sauce

Curried Cockchafers

Fricassee of Chicken with Chrysalids

Boiled Neck of Mutton with Wireworm Sauce

Ducklings with Green Peas

Cauliflowers garnished with Caterpillars

Moths on Toast

The noninsect aspects of this menu, incidentally, nicely reflect the eating habits of the Victorians!

Entomologists, understandably, have sometimes experimented with different ways of cooking insects and reported on the results in entomological journals. During the First World War, L. O. Howard, the leading American entomologist, strongly advocated the use of insects as one way of relieving the food shortage. He and his friends tried various recipes and published their findings in the *Journal of Economic Entomology*. Among other things, a stew of May beetle grubs was said to "taste agreeably like lobster."

My father-in-law, David Fairchild, famous for his work in introducing new plants into this country and always willing to experiment with new and interesting food, was infected by Howard's enthusiasm. One of my wife's earliest memories is of the time when her father decided the family had better get over prejudice and start eating grasshoppers. He fried the grasshoppers in sugar, but even that did not help with the children. The experiment was not a success and it took great will power on my wife's part to try eating grasshoppers again. She still does not really like them. The moral, I suppose, is that it is all right to experiment with cocktail guests, but be careful with your children.

V ❦ Sex: Male, Female, Other

> But after all, these things being done secretly, and the mind of the man being fickle, how can it be known what any person will do at any particular time and for any particular purpose?
>
> *The Kama Sutra of Vatsyayana,*
> in the translation of Sir Richard Burton

I T I S thus difficult to explain human food habits in terms of logic or reason or need; and this is equally true of sex habits. In the first place, man is peculiar among animals in his continuous sexuality—or at least his capability as an adult of developing a sexual response almost anytime. To be sure, this is equally true of dogs and other domestic animals—but only of the males. With the human animal, sexual impulses have lost specific timing in both males and females.

Most animals simply could not afford the sort of continuous sexuality that characterizes man: they are too busy finding food, defending themselves, getting about in the world, to be constantly preoccupied with sex. Sexual behavior throughout the animal kingdom is strictly directed toward reproductive ends: the female is receptive to males only when the sperm can be utilized, usually when ova are ready for fertilization. In a great many animals, physiological events are closely timed in both sexes, so that males are potent and sexually active only at the time when the female of the species is receptive. In high latitudes the timing of sexual activity is generally governed by seasonal changes, like the lengthening or shortening of the period of daylight. But the timing of sexual activity may be equally precise in the more uniform environment of the midtropics, where it is difficult to see how events in the two sexes can be so neatly synchronized.

Insects represent an extreme of sexual economy. Many species are parthenogenetic; that is, the eggs of the females develop without fertilization. In some cases males seem to have been dispensed with entirely—at least no males have ever been found—while in other cases males appear only occasionally. Insect females, with rare exceptions, have an organ called the spermatheca, in which supplies of sperm can be stored. Thus a queen bee or queen ant needs to mate only once, acquiring a supply of sperm that lasts for years. Insect males have only a transitory importance.

My idea about the general tendency in nature to economize on sexual activities meets difficulties, especially in the elaborate mating rituals of some of the birds, which require the expenditure of a great amount of energy and time on the part of the males at least. The extreme is reached by the bowerbirds of Australia and New Guinea. The males of some species spend months clearing a small patch of forest floor and building an elaborate structure ornamented with all sorts of bright-colored oddments like snail shells, beetles, seeds, pebbles, feathers and fruits. Flowers may be used, replaced as they fade. In Australia where the birds live near people, keys, glass, jewelry and bits of bright metal may be added to the collection of ornaments. The late Thomas Gilliard, an ornithologist who made a special study of these birds, estimated in one case that about three thousand sticks had been used in building the bower, and nearly a thousand objects in ornamenting it.

The male bowerbird, it appears, has functioning testes

all during the four or five months that he may spend in building and maintaining the bower. The female, on the other hand, is sexually inactive during much of this time, and the function of the bower is to arouse her, after which it serves as a mating station. The bower, built by relatively plain birds, thus seems to take the place of the gaudy plumage in male birds of other species. But it certainly does not represent an economy of energy in arriving at sexual fulfillment; on the contrary, it has been suggested that the bower building forms an outlet for an excess of energy—a form of conspicuous waste.

The anatomical structures developed by the males of some animals form another blow to the theory of economy. The extreme here seems to me to be the antlers of the members of the deer tribe. They are shed every year, to be regrown for the next rutting season at what must be considerable physiological cost to the animal. Antlers reached the height of absurdity in the extinct Irish deer—antlers measuring twelve feet across have been found. The purpose remains obscure. Short, sharp horns like those of cattle would make more efficient weapons. And while carcasses of male deer with antlers entangled are found occasionally, indicating death from fights, serious injury is rare. Fighting among deer, as among most animals, is largely a matter of harmless, ritual bluff. Maybe the big antlers serve well for bluffing; or perhaps they serve to impress the female. But, again, whatever their function, they could hardly be called economical.

Structures like the antlers of deer, and behavior like that of bowerbirds, are what biologists call secondary sexual characters, as distinguished from the primary structures and behavior involved in the copulatory act itself. The human animal has secondary sexual anatomical traits, such as the male beard, and he engages in a great deal of secondary sexual behavior, e.g., getting flowers for his date and taking her to a dance. But he also engages in a great deal of primary sexual activity not directed toward reproduction, and this I believe is unique. The late Raymond Pearl made a study of 199 married couples in Baltimore —apparently normal, healthy people who did not practice contraception. He found, on the average, that there were 351 copulations between these couples for each pregnancy. Monkeys in the zoo sometimes carry on outrageously, but no animal in the wild indulges in this much useless sexual activity.

In general copulation occurs in wild animals only when the female can use the sperm: usually when the eggs are ripe for fertilization. Among insects, as we have seen, the sperm can be stored and this is often true of cold-blooded animals, but it is also true of hibernating bats, which mate in the fall, the females holding the sperm over the winter for fertilization toward spring. Female mammals generally have a period of estrus, or heat, a time of sexual excitement and receptivity; this usually corresponds with ovulation, but in some cases (cats and rabbits, for instance) copulation serves as the immediate stimulus for ovulation.

Many attempts have been made to find traces of estrus behavior in the human female—usually by the questionnaire method of asking a large number of women at what stage in the monthly cycle they feel most sexual desire. But as far as I know, no one has been able to demonstrate any significant increase in desire at the time of ovulation, and many women report that they are most easily aroused at quite inappropriate times, like immediately before or after menstruation. Folk beliefs about conception, incidentally, are usually erroneous. In man, then, whether or not the egg gets fertilized is a matter of sheer accident. When one looks at the odds—the short time the ovum is ripe for fertilization, the long and hazardous journey that the microscopic sperm must make, the immense number of sperm needed to insure that one arrives—it seems unlikely that any human female will ever become pregnant. Yet it happens all the time.

How did man develop this peculiar sexuality? The fossil record offers no help in answering this question. We can sometimes get glimmerings about food habits from materials left in caves or around campsites, but there is nothing to indicate sex habits. For a given fossil type we have no way of knowing whether the females had an estrus phenomenon; whether they were monogamous, polygamous or promiscuous; or whether the males were possessive and jealous. Nor are comparative studies of contemporary peoples helpful. Different societies show an extraordinary variety of sexual customs, but the differences are clearly a consequence of culture, of the traditionally inherited ideas of each society. Physiologically, living humans are all the same kind of animal.

Perhaps suggestive ideas could be acquired from comparative animal studies, particularly of the behavior of nonhuman primates. The most detailed studies however are necessarily made with captive animals, and I tend to view this research with considerable suspicion. It is like trying to understand human behavior from studies in a model prison: the behavior is apt to be aberrant even if individuals of both sexes are confined together in the study jail. There is the effect of confinement itself: inability to move out, loss of freedom to choose associates. And then there is the curious effect of human control on animals. An experimental psychologist, for instance, can make almost any mammal develop neurotic behavior in the laboratory, but it is hard to imagine animal neurosis in a state of nature.

We are now gradually accumulating some very fine studies of primate behavior based on the observation of wild animals, with results often in direct conflict with ideas based on the study of captives. The first of the detailed field studies of primates were made by C. R. Carpenter on howler monkeys in Panama and gibbons in Thailand. More recently, the mountain gorilla in Africa has been studied by George Schaller, chimpanzees independently by Jane Goodall and Vernon Reynolds, baboons by Irven DeVore and Sherwood Washburn, the Japanese macaques by a group of local scientists, and so on.

In all species sex seems to be far less important among wild animals than among captive ones: after all, there isn't much else for animals in a cage to do. Sex plays a more prominent part in the lives of baboons and macaques in the wild than in the case of other species—and this is also true of these animals in captivity. But the jealousy and fighting among males that characterizes zoo animals is much less apparent in the wild.

The studies of gorillas and chimpanzees are most interesting from our point of view, because these animals are the most closely related to man. I think our idea of the jealous Old Man kicking out his sons when they become a sexual threat to him is largely based on the way we think gorillas ought to act. Big, fierce, hairy brutes: they must be continually preoccupied with sex. George Schaller's careful observations of gorillas in the wild over a period of almost two years give no support to this at all. Gorillas in fact turn out to be the most peaceable of animals: the most serious expression of aggression among adult males takes the form of trying to stare each other down. The only squabbling Schaller noticed within bands was among females, but "the grappling, screaming and mock biting never resulted in discernible injury . . . Twice the dominant male stopped the squabbling by merely walking toward the fighting animals and emitting annoyed grunts."

Schaller had little opportunity to observe sexual behavior in gorillas for the simple reason that sex plays a very trivial part in their lives. He observed copulation only twice. In each case the female took the initiative in approaching a male of her choice. Copulation was accompanied by special cries not heard otherwise, and the action was not in the least surreptitious. In the case of the first copulation observed, Schaller noted that "In spite of these far from silent doings, none of the other members of the group paid the slightest attention. Even Big Daddy, the boss, who rested in full view of the copulators, was seemingly oblivious of the spectacle." So much for the jealous Old Man. The dominant male of a group, it appeared, asserted his authority chiefly when he wanted some particularly comfortable resting spot or some choice morsel of food.

Chimpanzees have a quite different social organization from that of gorillas. The gorilla bands are stable over long periods of time. The smallest group observed by Schaller included five individuals; the largest, twenty-seven. Each band ranged over a fairly definite area. The areas frequently overlapped and two bands would sometimes come into contact with each other, but they never merged, and intermingled only briefly. The chimpanzee groups, on the other hand, have been found by all observers to be very fluid; they form and re-form easily, the number of individuals in a group seeming to depend largely on the availability of food. There is no dominant male leading a group: the bands sometimes consist only of males, and sometimes only of females with young. Every sort of age and sex combination occurs. But as with gorillas, no signs of sexual jealousy have been encountered among chimps.

With chimps the female sometimes takes the initiative, but more often it is the male. No male however shows any sexual interest in a female unless she is in estrus. The permissive chimpanzee attitude toward sex is nicely shown in the following account by Vernon and Frances Reynolds: "Four adult males and an estrous female . . . comprised the group. The female was grooming an adult male, and the male showed an erection. The male moved away a little, and the female followed him. She lay down on her belly on the branch in front of him and he copulated with her for a few seconds in a sitting position (from 10 to 15 thrusts), then sat a few yards off, picking off the ejaculate. A second male approached the female and groomed her, while a third manipulated his own erect penis. A little while later, three of the males were grooming each other and the female had moved off."

From the point of view of sexual economy, masturbation and homosexuality are the most wasteful human practices, since the objective of reproduction is never achieved. Completely efficient contraception would also have to be classed here; but this is too recent a development for there to be any question about its history.

Masturbation—according to Kinsey and also according to everyone's experience—is practically universal in our culture among males and quite common among females. Statistics for other societies are hard to come by, but one can presume that all young humans try manipulating their genitals, though in cultures permissive toward heterosexual intercourse for adolescents the habit may not persist. Homosexuality is not universal in our culture, but Kinsey's questioning showed that it is surprisingly common. Furthermore, the sort of survey reported by Clelland Ford and Frank Beach in their book on *Patterns of Sexual Behavior* shows that it probably occurs in all cultures, and that in some cultures every male goes through homosexual experiences. We have evidence of homosexual practices as far back in history as there are written or pictorial records for civilizations, so that we can presume that it has been a human practice for a long time.

Masturbation and homosexual behavior have often enough been observed among captive animals, and this is sometimes used as an argument that such behavior is "natural." If such practices were really widespread outside of captivity, one could suppose that the corresponding human

behavior was a biological rather than a cultural development—though I wouldn't want to argue that biology is
natural and culture not. But reports of nonreproductive
sexual behavior leading to ejaculation among animals in
the wild are too sporadic and too special to form the basis
of any general theory.

Schaller states flatly that he saw no signs of homosexual
behavior among his wild gorillas, nor of erotic play among
the young. In the case of chimpanzees I have not come
across any account of mutual stimulation between males or
between females that seemed to have as its objective sexual
fulfillment—what I suppose could be called overt homosexuality—though the males are often affectionate enough
with one another, as shown by my quotation from observations by the Reynoldses.

Among both baboons and the Japansese macaques, young
males may show submissive, female-like attitudes toward
older, dominant males, and may even be mounted by such
males. But this seems to be a sort of ritual act of submission. Intromission seems not to occur, so that the goal of
the behavior is not so much sexual satisfaction for either
male, as it is an expression of the dominance hierarchy
within the group. The behavior of caged animals shows
that these monkeys are perfectly capable of truly homosexual behavior, with intromission in the anus and ejaculation—apparently with satisfaction for all concerned.

Wild primates often become involved with the manipulation of their own genitals; but I would think this should
not be called masturbation unless it leads to ejaculation.
Certainly, however, odd behavior patterns do occur. A
friend who has just returned from a visit to the African
parks tells me that the male baboons in one of the parks
become sexually excited by automobiles, jump on the
hood, and ejaculate on the windshield.

The members of the deer tribe develop a powerful sexual drive during their rutting season and in some cases the

males become sexually active two weeks or so before the females come into heat, leading to a variety of forms of autoerotic behavior. Fraser Darling, in his classic study of *A Herd of Red Deer* in Scotland, found that the hardened antlers of these deer apparently form a sensitive erotic zone. He described what might be called antler masturbation as follows:

"This act is accomplished by lowering the head and gently drawing the tips of the antlers to and fro through the herbage. Erection and extrusion of the penis from the sheath follow in five to seven seconds. There is but little protrusion and retraction of the penis and no oscillating movements of the pelvis. Ejaculation follows about five seconds after the penis is erected, so that the whole act takes ten to fifteen seconds. These antlers, used now so delicately, may within a few minutes be used with all the body's force behind them to clash with the antlers of another stag. These mysterious organs are a paradox; at one moment exquisitely sensitive, they can be apparently without feeling the next."

Neither the behavior of the deer or the baboons nor the occasional other kinds of autoerotic behavior observed in the wild would seem to have much relevance to human behavior. Because of the frequency with which unusual sexual habits are developed by captive primates, I have sometimes wondered whether man's sexuality was a consequence of confinement. In our houses and cities we live in cages. Still, we are far from being confined in the sense that monkeys are in a zoo or an experimental laboratory. Further, unusual sexual behavior is not limited to houses and cities: the wildest tribes, living in apparent harmony with the rest of nature, show sexual patterns that are quite different from those of the animals among which they live. Maybe the human confinement is not due to physical walls, but to culture: every individual lives within the cage of his culture, confined by bars of tradition an/

custom that restrict actions as strongly, if not as obviously, as the bars of the zoo. This sounds nice, but I don't think it works as an explanation of the unusual aspects of human sexuality.

Perhaps it is more reasonable to think that man, in the course of cultural development, has lost the need for sexual economy imposed on most animals by their way of life. Man has become secure enough so that he can afford to indulge in heterosexual copulation when the female is not in estrus, or take up homosexuality or autoeroticism or other nonreproductive forms of sexual behavior.

Through the development of culture, man has escaped to some degree the rigid controls of natural selection that govern behavior in the rest of nature. He is still subject to a wide variety of selective forces, but the forces that govern whether a man survives and reproduces are in many ways different from those that govern the survival of a fox, a crocodile or even a gorilla. Man's situation is most similar to that of his domesticated animals and plants: they too have come to be protected and governed by cultural developments, with at least some of the pressures of natural selection released or altered. It has been suggested that we might well look at man as a "self-domesticated animal."

Domestication implies essentially a controlled and readily available food supply, protection from natural enemies, and selection for traits according to human whims or needs—the replacement of natural selection by artificial selection. These all apply to man. Like his domesticated species, man shows a wide range of variability in such instances as skin color, hair texture and size: comparable variability is not found in any wild species. Males of most domesticated animals, like the human male, have lost sexual periodicity and are able and willing to mate at any ~ne. But estrus still occurs in the females of domesticated and they are receptive to male attentions only periodically. The human female remains unique among mammals—and not easily explained.

It can be argued that the essence of the idea of domestication is the control of one species by another, which makes "self-domestication" meaningless, though thought-provoking. The basis of the comparison, as we have seen, is that both man and his domesticated animals have escaped some of the usual controls of nature. But if we look for the basis of man's escape, we find it in the cooperative behavior of social groups, and in the development of language and thought and the consequent improved ability to accumulate information and to pass it on through the process of teaching and learning. The unusual thing here is the teaching: a dog can learn many tricks, but his ability to teach is limited. Historically man first developed some degree of control over himself and then extended it to a series of other organisms. It might be more logical, then, instead of calling man "self-domesticated," to call the animals associated with him "acculturated," since their fate has fallen under the control of cultural forces. But this is getting away from sex.

It seems likely, as I remarked in an earlier chapter, that the form of sexual behavior in man and in the great apes is largely learned: at least captive chimpanzees, raised in isolation, seem not to know what to do when placed with a female in estrus. Jane Goodall was able to observe this learning process in the course of her field studies, noticing infants on six occasions watching carefully when their mothers were copulating. "On one occasion an infant went close, peered intently underneath its mother, reached out one hand and felt in the region where the penis was inserted into the vagina."

There are other lines of evidence for the dominance of learning, rather than instinctive or endocrine control, in the case of man. Kinsey and others report that males castrated as adults continue to respond sexually and are a to copulate normally even though the sexual endocrine system has been disrupted. The same is true of the female after the removal of the ovaries.

Then too there is clear evidence of learning in the great variety of copulatory positions adopted by humans, and the different kinds of sexual approaches developed by different cultures. *The Kama Sutra of Vatsyayana* lists some twenty possible positions for sexual congress (the phrase used in Sir Richard Burton's translation), and while certainly thorough, the *Kama Sutra* hardly exhausts all possibilities. Mating behavior with most animals is quite stereotyped: it varies greatly from species to species, but individuals of any given species act in much the same way.

In Western civilization we tend to regard kissing and manipulation of the breasts as natural approaches to direct sexual activity. But in many other cultures the breasts have no erotic interest, and the idea of kissing may be viewed with horror. We tend also to think that the natural way to copulate is lying down, face-to-face, with the male on top; other positions are sought for the sake of variety or by way of experiment, and are often accompanied by a vague unease at unnatural behavior or the thrill of novelty. But this natural way of Western civilization may seem quite strange to peoples of other cultures. I have read somewhere that in the Pacific Islands our usual sexual position came to be known as "missionary fucking" because it was a new idea to the islanders. The missionaries, incidentally, may have thought they were being discreet about sex, but it is difficult to hide any aspect of behavior on a small Pacific island.

Sexual play is common among the young in most human societies—sometimes with adult approval, sometimes not —and this is surely an important part of the learning ~cess. With man one can never discount the importance ~ learning, and almost everyone likes to talk about ~oviding a ready means of transmitting sex information between generations and among members of peer groups. In many cases, too, there is formal sex instruction or initiation. Adults in most societies tend to be more or less surreptitious about sexual activity, but even so the curious young often get a chance to look, and this may be important in learning. In some societies, I am told, the older males introduce young females into the mysteries of sex, and older females the young males. To aging males in our culture this might seem more and more an ideal arrangement for maintaining tradition, but I don't know that it is very common.

Behavior that is learned may be learned faultily, and this accounts for the variety of bizarre practices that have become associated with sex in man. Psychologists have a substantial catalogue of aberrations or perversions: sadism, masochism, voyeurism, fetishism, and a considerable variety of homosexual and autoerotic practices. It seems to me most likely that these are the consequence of sexual satisfactions found by individuals in the process of growing up. But given the experimental tendencies of juvenile humans, the wonder is that anyone grows up to conform to the norm of his (or her) culture. That each culture does have a norm seems to me testimony of the universal pressures for conformity.

The human species, then, is characterized by a continuous sexuality which may start well before puberty and last into old age. The intensity of the sexual drive is influenced by hormones, but the form of sexual expression is learned. This is shown nicely by attempts to cure male homosexuals through the injection of testosterone: the urge to sexual activity was increased, but its direction was not changed.

The continuous and often diffuse sexuality undoubtedly has all sorts of consequences in human social organization, but cause-and-effect relations are hard to isolate because of cultural diversity. Sexual awareness and attraction are surely strong cohesive forces, keeping members of groups together. I, and many others, have wondered whether the readiness with which human males cooperate in small groups, in hunting, in war, or in building their societies, might not be due to a sort of general, subthreshold homosexual tendency. Cooperation among adult males was, it seems to me, essential for the beginning of human social organization and this implies some bond of mutual attraction and esteem. On the other hand, male gorillas and chimpanzees get along with each other well enough, though there is no evidence for inter-male sexual attraction.

Sex can also be a disruptive force, leading to jealousy and conflict. When H. G. Wells tried to imagine a ruthlessly efficient Martian society in *The War of the Worlds,* he had his octopus-like Martians reproduce by budding. They thus avoided the distractions and dissensions that sometimes seem an inevitable accompaniment of the sexual process.

With the social insects, sex has been almost completely eliminated, involving only a few members of the species for brief periods of time. This makes possible a very tight social organization within the colony, with the behavior of each individual completely subordinate to the needs of the group as a whole. It may well be that human sexuality, tending to be both a cohesive and a divisive force, makes such tight organization impossible. If this is true, sex is the basis of the individualism of which we in the Western tradition are so proud. Individualism is unthinkable in the case of a sterile, worker ant.

The ant colony is a gigantic family, all of its members the offspring of a single reproductive individual, the queen. With man, the simplest sorts of social organization that we know involve both families and larger groups, tribes. One can easily get into long arguments about which was first, the family or the tribe: whether tribal groupings represent the union of several families, or whether the family somehow came to be formed within the larger group. In other words, one can argue about whether man was originally monogamous, polygamous or promiscuous. In a way this narrows down to a question of whether man is naturally family-oriented or whether he (or she) is naturally promiscuous and sexual restrictions are imposed by the culture.

I think that the majority of anthropologists and psychologists nowadays consider the nuclear family to be the basic unit of human organization: that tribes were formed by groups of families somehow coming to be associated. Certainly some sort of family structure is universal among contemporary peoples, and the family unit must have a long history.

But I still cannot believe that the nuclear family was the primitive or original pattern of human or prehuman organization. The social primates are all promiscuous: there are no long-term sexual associations between particular males and females within the group. Baboons and macaques show sexual rivalry—that is, dominant males take precedence in sex. But as we have seen, who copulates with whom seems to be a matter of complete indifference among gorillas and chimpanzees. The gorilla pattern of forming small groups seems to me the most likely parallel to the formation of social organization among the protohominids.

Of course the fact that gorillas and chimps are sexually promiscuous is no proof that the protohominids were; men and apes have been evolving independently for millions of years. And among the apes, the gibbons show a strictly family organization: the groups consist of one adult male, one female, and one or two young—and the sexual association between the adults seems to be for life. But a gibbon-like organization would hardly be possible among the protohominids. The animals in the human line have long been rather feeble creatures, with no special armament of tooth or claw, and utterly lacking in the acrobatic skill which keeps the vegetarian gibbons relatively safe from enemies. Man is powerful—and safe—only when acting cooperatively in larger-than-family groups. The family, then, must have formed somehow within the group.

How family structure started I cannot imagine, though I can see the value of it for the human bands. When the human female lost the sexual control of estrus, sexual behavior would have gained a significance quite different from that which it has in the life of gorillas and chimps, where sex seems to be a transient and unimportant matter in the lives of the animals. With continuous sexuality, some sort of family structure would seem to be necessary to avoid chaos, to make the sexual activity a constructive and cohesive force instead of a destructive one.

If the theory that the family was formed within the group is correct, sexual jealousy would seem to be something learned from the culture rather than an inborn human trait. The great range of attitudes toward sexual fidelity shown by different human societies lends support to this idea. The horror of incest would then also seem to be a consequence of cultural learning rather than an expression of an innate behavioral attitude, and this indeed seems to be the case.

VI ❧ Incest and Cannibalism

> Traditional morality owes a great deal to savage superstition, but that merely proves that a great deal of traditional morality is superstitious, not that savage superstition is moral.
>
> ROBERT BRIFFAULT,
> *Sin and Sex*

CANNIBALISM IS the strongest food taboo in the modern Western world. We are, to be sure, horrified at the idea of eating many things—for instance, dogs, worms or insects, as mentioned earlier; and we are disgusted by the thought of coprophagy—the elegant term for eating shit. But eating people is the worst of all. This in spite of the fact that we all know that cannibalism in various forms has been practiced by many different societies, and in our own society under stress. But we think of it as a savage and repugnant custom, characteristic of tribes that have not yet encountered the blessings of civilization.

Incest similarly has a preeminent place among our sex taboos, though it is not quite so clearly our greatest horror. Sex murders of children would surely take first place among horrors, but I think it would be misleading to call such murder a taboo. Then there is rape: laws in our society are far more severe about rape than about incest, and the law is supposed to reflect social custom. Prohibition of rape also might be considered outside the range of taboos, except that there are societies in which you are supposed to get your gal in the first place by raping her.

Adultery also comes to mind. It is supposed to be deplorable behavior, despite Dr. Kinsey's statistics on the frequency of extramarital intercourse in the United States. Referring to law again, wherever divorce is allowed in the Western world, adultery is considered to be valid grounds. According to our mores, at least, it is often thought proper for a man to shoot his wife's lover if he catches him in the act—which would seem to indicate pretty strong condemnation of adultery. But I don't think the idea of adultery produces in us the same queasy feeling that the idea of incest does.

There is, further, the nice question whether the taboo against incest or the taboo against perversion is stronger. I would guess that homosexual behavior in our society is much more common than incest, which would at least indicate a more easily broken taboo, but I know of no statistics. The Kinsey workers so far have been reticent about their figures on incest, only noting that they have a "very small" number of cases for adolescent or older males. One way of looking at it would be to ask whether it is a greater insult to call a man a motherfucker or a cocksucker, but I haven't come across any experiments designed to answer this. I certainly shall not try asking the question—it is easy enough to start a fight with either term.

Incest, whatever its relative status as a horror, has acquired a very special significance among possible sexual behavior patterns, in part because of Freud's discovery of the Oedipus complex. Psychological questionnaires generally probe into feelings about mother and father. The clinical psychologists find traces of Oedipus in the dark subconscious of every man: poor, blinded Oedipus, endlessly pursued by the Furies because he unwittingly killed his father and wed his mother, is a symbol of conflict for all of us. It seems to me that the infantile experience would be more apt to lead you to want to eat your mother rather than to copulate with her, though I must admit that I have come across no cases of mother-eating, even in mythology. There are a number of instances of gods being tricked into eating their children—as in the case of Chronos—but the psychologists seem to have made nothing of this.

It is often said that the incest taboo is the only cultural trait common to all human societies. Incest, like gravitation, thus acquires the fascination of a universal law. There is a derivative belief that since the incest taboo is universal, it must have some single, universal explanation. A great deal of effort has gone into the search for this explanation, but it remains elusive. There are dozens of theories, often defended with great vigor by their proponents, but none has really gained general acceptance. Some of the theories are in direct conflict. It has been maintained, for instance, that the human species has an "instinctive" horror of sexual relations within the nuclear family, among people who have grown up from infancy together, and that this horror is reflected in the taboo. But other students have thought that the human tendency would be to mate within the family, with the most familiar individuals, if this were not prohibited. The idea is that intra-family mating would disrupt smooth relationships; hence the universal need to combat the urge with strong taboos or regulations.

The definitions of incest and the explanations of incest taboos are so diverse that I have gradually come to feel that perhaps the universal incest taboo exists chiefly in the minds of social scientists. Some form of social regulation of marriage seems to be universal; that is, all peoples have ideas about the kinds of individuals who can properly have sexual relations with each other, and all peoples have some way of insuring that infants will be properly cared for. Furthermore, all societies have some system of classifying different degrees of kinship, and quite "simple" societies like those of the Australian aborigines may have very complex kinship classifications. It thus seems natural enough that the customs or rules governing marriage would include kinship restrictions or preferences —and violation of the restrictions is what we call incest. The kinds of kin forbidden to intermarry differ greatly from society to society, which makes "incest" seem to be a wastebasket word in which a variety of sins has been collected. Wastebaskets are notoriously confused.

One can narrow down the meaning of kin to the nuclear family, and say that father-daughter, mother-son, and brother-sister sexual relations form the core of incest taboos. But even these are not universal. There are the well-known cases of brother-sister marriages in such royal lines as the Pharaohs and Ptolemies of Egypt, the Incas of Peru and the Hawaiian royal family. In the lines of certain African chiefs, father-daughter and mother-son unions were said to occur. All of these exceptions, of course, can be taken to show that the behavior of royalty, like that of gods, is not subject to ordinary rules. But the exceptions are not confined to royalty.

J. S. Slotkin, in an article published in the *American Anthropologist* in 1947, presented evidence showing that there were no incest prohibitions in ancient Persia: that mother-son and father-daughter marriages occurred, as well as marriages between brothers and sisters. There is also a great deal of evidence, summarized by Russell Middleton in an article in the issue of the *American Sociological Review* for October 1962, showing that brother-sister marriages were quite common in Egypt in Ptolemaic and Roman times. They may also have been common earlier, but evidence about the lives of ordinary people under the Pharaohs is scanty. Middleton thinks that these marriages were a convenient way of maintaining family property. They were prohibited for Roman citizens, though allowed for Egyptians. Marriages between half brothers and half sisters—siblings with the same father but different mothers—are allowed in quite a number of different societies.

One gets the impression that the horror of incest is particularly strong in the modern Western world, and that this is an aspect of the general antisex bias of the Christian tradition. The Christian prohibitions, of course, can be traced back to the Judaic rules of conduct; and since sex and religion are often related, many Judeo-Christian attitudes can be looked upon as reactions against heathen practices. But the roots of the Western attitude toward sex are deep and complex and any attempt at summary is bound to be an oversimplification. The subject has been explored in many books, and I have cited some of them in the notes at the back of this one.

Among Christian sects, the only one I know of that sanctioned incest was the Mormon. The Mormon justification was based on the example of Adam and Eve and their children. But both incest and polygamy were in the end prohibited by laws passed in 1892 by the Utah Legislature, and this particular heresy was brought into line with the general tradition of our culture.

The early Church Fathers went to extremes in defining incest: marriage was prohibited even between sixth cousins. The idea seems to have been to prevent marriage between any persons' who could claim any blood relationship. Even "spiritual relationships" fell under the incest rules. The famous code of the Emperor Justinian included a provision that a man could not marry a woman for whom he had stood godfather in baptism, and this was later extended to include such relationships as a godfather and a sister of the godchild.

Surely these elaborate rules were not carefully observed. In a small and settled medieval village almost everyone would be related in some way to everyone else; and even in such villages people could hardly keep track of relationships to the seventh degree. Besides, the difference between what people actually do and what they think they ought to do is often profound—as Kinsey has shown.

But why is some sort of incest taboo so general? There does not seem to me to be any evidence for an innate or instinctive basis for aversion to sexual relations between siblings or between parents and offspring. On the contrary, sex between young and adolescent familiars would seem more likely than sexual experimentation with strangers. If human incest avoidance had a deep-seated behavioral basis, one would expect to find evidence of such aversion among other primates, such as gorillas and chimps. But there does not even seem to be any mechanism for siblings or parents and offspring to recognize each other after they have grown up. Among animals, the only instance I know of behavior similar to our incest avoidance is among geese. With the Canada goose, for instance, siblings simply will not mate with one another. But any behavioral similarities between people and geese are surely matters of coincidence.

It is often said that close inbreeding was avoided by early man because he observed the unfortunate genetic consequences. Certainly many harmful genetic traits are recessive; that is, they do not show ordinarily because they are masked by a corresponding trait (called an allele by geneticists) that is either neutral or beneficial. Related individuals are likely to have the same recessive traits, which would then be brought out by inbreeding. But the opinion of most modern geneticists seems to be that inbreeding among people would not lead to any more obviously defective offspring than does random mating, so that untoward genetic consequences of incest could hardly have been observed by our primitive ancestors. After all, Cleopatra was the product of several generations of brother-sister marriages, and she seems to have had no physical defects.

One idea, as I mentioned before, is that if sexual relations were allowed within the nuclear family—except of course between the parents—the family unit would become disrupted by discord and jealousy. I don't know how one could test this without making some experiments, which is hardly possible. There are many cases of incest reported in the psychological and legal literature, and these instances often involve disrupted families. But such cases come to light because an individual has been arrested or has sought psychiatric treatment. Where incestuous relations were peaceful and happy they would be far less likely to come to the attention of either the law or psychology—they would have to be uncovered by Kinsey-like sleuthing.

To me the most reasonable theory is one that was first proposed by E. B. Tylor—generally considered the father of modern anthropology—back in 1888, and in recent times most vigorously espoused by Leslie White, a distinguished anthropologist at the University of Michigan. Essentially, Tylor's theory is that marrying outside the family increased security by widening the bonds of relationship. As Tylor put it, "Again and again in the world's history, savage tribes must have had plainly before their minds the simple practical alternative between marrying out and being killed out. . . ."

I like the explanation given to Margaret Mead by one of the old men of the Arapesh people of New Guinea, and reported in her book *Sex and Temperament in Three Primitive Societies*. "What," the old man said in answer to a question by one of the young men, "you would like to marry your sister! What is the matter with you anyway? Don't you want a brother-in-law? Don't you realize that if you marry another man's sister and another man marries your sister, you will have at least two brothers-in-law, while if you marry your own sister you will have none? With whom will you hunt, with whom will you garden, whom will you go to visit?"

Whatever the explanation of the taboo for ordinary humans, incestuous relations appear to be regarded as perfectly natural for gods by many different peoples. Among the Egyptians, for instance, the sisters Isis and Nephthys married their brothers, Osiris and Set. In Hindu mythology, Yama, King of the Dead, married his sister Wami; and in the Vedic hymns there is a case of an incestuous homosexual relationship between the twin brothers Varuna and Mitra. The world creators of Japanese mythology, Izanagi and Izanami, were brother and sister; among other things, they were responsible for the invention of sexual intercourse.

The Greek and Roman gods, as we all know, carried on scandalously—at least in terms of modern Western ideas about morals, though these gods were the creations of our intellectual ancestors. Zeus himself was the son of an incestuous union between Rhea and her brother Chronos; and his activities included the rape of his mother, Rhea; marriage with his sister, Hera; and sexual relations with his daughter Persephone, the offspring of his rape of Demeter.

So we find all possible patterns of incest among the immortals, carried out with seeming blitheness and with no untoward consequences. Zeus, to be sure, not only loved his mother, but hated his father, Chronos, and cast him out of Olympus, thus acting out the dark subconscious tendency that Sigmund Freud later found in every man. But it is difficult to fit gods into ordinary family patterns; and when Freud wanted to name his mother-loving, father-hating impulse, he chose not immortal Zeus, but legendary Oedipus.

There is also a good deal of incest in the Bible. Genesis,

like most creation myths, starts with incest: Adam and Eve and their children. The text is vague about how Adam's children found mates, but one presumes that they mated with one another since there weren't any other people around. The consequences of biblical incest are sometimes untoward, sometimes not. In the famous case of Lot and his daughters it seems to have been all right, since their children multiplied mightily. The extenuating circumstances may have been that the daughters got their father drunk before lying with him—though the principle that an action carried out while drunk is all right would seem to be a dubious morality. Then there is the case of Ham, who apparently had homosexual relations with his father, Noah, while Noah was drunk. The consequences of that action were that Ham's children were condemned to unending slavery. It is not clear, however, whether this fate depended on the incest, the homosexuality, or both. At any rate the fact that Noah was drunk didn't help Ham any.

To me then it seems most likely that the horror of incest is learned from our culture, and is not part of our biological inheritance. This is even more obviously true of that other deep horror of ours—cannibalism. The fact that the incest taboo is very general, even if not quite universal, is used as an argument that it must have some innate basis. But no one could possibly argue that the man-eating taboo was universal and hence deeply instinctive. There are too many well-documented accounts of cultures in which the eating of human flesh has been openly sanctioned as a regular or an occasional practice.

Yet the taboo is strong enough so that most of us, I suspect, would die of starvation before we would eat each other. There are, of course, well-authenticated cases of cannibalism among Westerners at the point of starvation, but surely the cases of Westerners dying of starvation without resorting to cannibalism are more numerous

The best-known instance of cannibalism in the history of the United States is that of the Donner Party, making their way to California in the winter of 1846–47. Fifteen members of the party, ten men and five women, became snowbound in the Sierra Nevada in what is now known as Donner Pass. Their food lasted for five days; after four days more, someone suggested that they draw lots to see who would die to keep the others alive, but the idea was rejected. They decided to struggle on until someone died. The first to perish was Antonio, a Mexican; but before any move could be made to eat him, the party was overtaken by an extremely bad storm which put out their fire; they had to crouch together for two days under a blanket which became buried in snow. When the storm abated, four more (all men) were found dead. The living roasted some of the human flesh, and dried the rest to carry with them.

On the fourth of January, twenty days after they had started to cross the pass, they were again starving. The surviving European men decided to kill and eat the two Indians that were with them. But the Indians were warned and escaped, only to be found a couple of days later, nearly dead, when they were shot by one of the starving men. Finally, two men and all five women managed to reach a settlement on the edge of the Sacramento Valley, thirty-three days after their start into the snow.

The survivors were plunged into an immediate notoriety, and one can still debate the morality of their resorting to cannibalism. The logic that some should die so that the others may live, and that it should be decided by lot, seems reasonable enough in the abstract. But this alternative was rejected by the Donner Party (at least according to the record), except for the case of the two moribund Indians. That the first individuals dying should be eaten in order that the others might live seems even more reasonable, though I suppose there is no way of knowing whether or not one would be capable of this until put to the test. The taboo in our culture is very strong. It is interesting that all five women survived this ordeal, but only two of the ten men—another tribute to the toughness of the female of our species.

It is difficult to determine how widespread cannibalism has been in the human past. Western travelers, from the days of Herodotus down through those of Marco Polo and on to recent times, have tended to accuse barbarians of cannibal habits: cannibal and savage are closely related words in the European vocabulary. For this reason many accusations of cannibalism—or other "barbaric" practices—have to be discounted. But there are plenty of well-authenticated cases in all parts of the world in which cannibalism is an institutionalized or openly avowed custom. The practices are so diverse that it would seem either that cannibalism has arisen independently many times in human history or that people-eating is a very ancient human habit which has taken on many forms in the course of time—including complete suppression.

There is evidence of the ancientness of cannibalism in the paleontological record. In the case of the fossils of Pekin man, many of the long bones were split open, and the only likely explanation of this is that they were split by other men to get at the marrow. Man has long been particularly fond of marrow, which he gets by splitting bones; any other animal would have to chew them.

Each of the Pekin skulls also had a hole in its base—the foramen magnum, which is the weakest part of the skull, had been cut out to get at the brains. Contemporary headhunters often make a similar break to get at the brains of their victims, which are ceremonially eaten. A number of Neanderthal skulls have been found with this same kind of opening in the foramen magnum, and in these cases there is evidence from the position in which the skulls were found that the murder and cannibalism were involved in some kind of ritual.

Whether Pekin man indulged in ritual or just liked the taste of his own kind of meat we cannot tell. Among the cannibal tribes of modern times that have been studied by ethnologists, we find cases in which human flesh is eaten only for magical or religious reasons, and others in which the motives are more immediately practical: the meat is needed or prized as food.

There are, to be sure, many subvarieties of each of these categories. In the case of magical cannibalism, one may acquire strength by eating parts of a courageous enemy or gain other special mental or bodily characteristics of the slain. In the case of murder, eating a small part of the murdered man may ward off trouble from his ghost or may serve to prevent revenge by relatives. In religious ceremonies, ritual cannibalism and human sacrifice merge into the whole complex subject of sacrificial practices—which I would just as soon skip over.

In some parts of the world, but especially on many Pacific islands, man is simply the easiest available source of meat—and native reports also indicate that human flesh is tasty. Some peoples, like the pre-Columbian Caribs of America, waged war for the purpose of taking captives to be killed and eaten at some later time. I remember reading, while still in high school, about the Carib custom of breaking the legs of their Arawak captives so that they could not run away—a sort of primitive cold storage. My boyhood horror of the idea is still with me.

Some peoples eat only corpses, individuals that have been slain in battle or that have died from some other cause. As in the case of the Donner Party, this seems reasonable enough in the abstract. Maybe we could alleviate the meat shortages of wartime by adding the corpses of soldiers killed in battle to the meat supply. Horrible? Surely it is not as bad to eat someone already dead as it is to kill him in the first place.

In some cultures only friends are eaten; this, by analogy with in-marriage, or endogamy, is called "endocannibalism." In other cultures only enemies are eaten ("exocannibalism"). In the case of endocannibalism there may be rules similar to those governing incest: that is, parents may not eat their children or children their parents, or brothers their sisters, and so forth. A similar attitude shows in the etiquette of cannibalism in the Donner Party: "They observed one last sad propriety; no member of a family touched his own dead."

Ronald Berndt, in a recently published book, *Excess and Restraint*, has given a detailed account of cannibal practices among a group of New Guinea mountain people, where government and missions have only recently succeeded in suppressing the custom—or at least in driving it underground. These people were quite blithe about eating human flesh, regarding it simply as a readily available source of meat, otherwise hard to come by except for their few pigs—there are no large native mammals in New Guinea. They ate both their enemies and their friends without any special ceremony or magical involvement— though they only ate their friends after the friends had died from disease or accident. Food and sex were sometimes neatly combined when the men would copulate with a female corpse before cutting it up for eating. They had one story of a man who got his penis cut off because he dallied too long for the patience of his hungry friends.

Often the corpses were buried for a few days and then dug up for feasting—the decayed flesh and accompanying maggots being regarded as special delicacies. What, for us, could be more disgusting? But these New Guinea people thought nothing of it. They liked the taste, their mothers had not taught them that rotten meat and worms were bad, their culture had no taboo on eating people.

This brings up the general question of disgust, aversion or abhorrence. I have gone through the indices of a number of general psychology books to check on these words, but either they are absent or the discussion is not very illuminating. If one digs further into psychological literature, one comes again across the debate about innate versus learned responses; there seem to be many strong opinions, but they are based on little clear evidence. Is shit naturally disgusting, or did we learn to think it so? My own feeling is that the disgust of particular materials or actions is always learned, though there may well be some innate general basis for aversion which gets channeled into different directions in the process of growing up in different cultures.

I stopped writing at this point to go into the kitchen for something, and noticed a bad smell. Tracking it down, I found some rotten meat in the cat's dish. I cleaned the thing out and took the mess down to the incinerator in the cellar, as disgusted by the whole process as anyone could be. I don't think I could possibly have forced myself to taste the meat, which had already acquired small maggots—though in New Guinea terms this stuff might well have been considered a delicacy. Sure, I learned my aversion in childhold—I was not born with a disgust for either rotten meat or worms. But it is sobering to find that, despite my brave talk, I am just as culture-bound as the next man.

We learn aversions; but if we try we can also learn to overcome them, though it is sometimes a slow process. I still remember my first exposure to high game—venison served me by an epicure whom I greatly admired; I didn't have the courage to refuse the stuff and show my provincial background. It was smelly enough so that it was hard to get past the nose; but I must admit that once in the mouth, it had a delicious taste. The problem with strong cheeses is similar; I only learned to eat them as an adult, but now I am very fond of them.

One psychologist who made a special study of disgust asked a considerable number of students to list the objects they found most disgusting. The things most often mentioned were feces, urine, secretions of the various mucous membranes, sweat and similar wastes of the human and animal body. It can be argued that this reaction is perfectly natural, based on an innate aversion to materials shed from the body, and especially to the reincorporation of such materials through the mouth. In this connection it is interesting that sputum is not particularly disgusting as long as it is in the mouth. We can swallow the stuff we cough up easily enough, but once it has been spat out our attitude changes completely.

Yet I think this attitude toward body wastes is learned. The infant certainly shows no aversion, playing with, even eating, his feces quite happily until horrified reactions from mother teach him to stop. The teaching and learning are quite easy in most cases, which may well indicate some sort of innate predisposition. Animals that are easily housebroken, like dogs and cats, do seem to have an instinctive tendency not to foul their lairs. It is difficult, if not impossible, to housebreak arboreal animals like monkeys and birds: they have no need for an instinctive basis for special disposition of bodily wastes, since they can simply drop them out of the trees.

Feces might well turn out to be the most common object of human disgust if one could make a cross-cultural survey, but I suspect that our disgust reaction is unusually strong, and an aversion to feces is not universal. Ronald Berndt, for instance, noted that the New Guinea cannibals that he studied often did not discard the feces of the corpses. He described one instance in which the feces of a man who had been shot were cut out with the belly and given to the man's wife, who ate them after cooking them, mixed with edible ferns and wrapped in banana leaves.

Our aversion to rotten meat—except for the British

aristocracy and their high game—is perhaps as strong as our aversion to feces. But until modern methods of refrigeration and preservation were developed, spoiled meat must have been common in diets, as it still is in many parts of the world. We say that we avoid spoiled meat because of the danger to health, but there seems to be little basis for this since food poisoning does not come from the decomposing bacteria. Decayed meat should be easier to digest than fresh—except that we do have difficulty digesting food we dislike, another instance of culture influencing physiology. As H. D. Renner remarks in his interesting little book on *The Origin of Food Habits,* "In such cases we are not thinking of our health, we only believe we are. Something stronger has come between our desire for food and our desire for self-preservation, something that unpsychological dietitians call prejudice, but which is as strong as taboo."

We can argue then that the New Guinea mountain people, in eating decayed corpses, are not being unnatural either because the meat is human or because it is rotten. Ethically I can see nothing wrong with eating humans who have died from "natural causes." There is a neat saying about this among the Cocomas Indians of the Amazon: "It is better to be inside a friend than to be swallowed up by the cold earth." The ethical problem, it seems to me, is in accepting killing people for the purpose of eating them. But killing other humans for food is only one of the immense variety of ways in which people manage to be mean to one another. Meanness is an outstanding human peculiarity—the psychologists call it aggression.

VII ॐ On Being Mean

> The great change in our world is that force isn't just (presumably) wrong, but plainly inexpedient.
>
> JOHN PAIRMAN BROWN,
> *The Displaced Person's Almanac*

SO FAR our chief preoccupation has been with food and sex. These are certainly important preoccupations for all adult humans, and for other kinds of animals as well. But they are not everything. People—and other animals—also spend a lot of time playing, fighting, working, sleeping, or just idling. But how can we classify these other activities? Nutrition and reproduction are easily recognized categories of behavior, and they are universals—every living thing must have some way of getting food, some way of reproducing its kind. Are there other universals?

I have spent a good deal of time with pencil and paper trying to work out a scheme for classifying behavior, but I have never managed to come up with anything very satisfactory, and none of the schemes used in textbooks has much appeal for me. Beyond food and sex, possible categories seem fuzzy and overlapping. My first thought for a third universal goal for behavior is survival. Every organism must have some way of avoiding, fighting, or deceiving possible enemies. Often some way must be found of coping with environment: building shelters, digging holes, or finding snug retreats. But food is also necessary for the survival of the individual, and sex or some other method of reproduction for the survival of the species, so that the distinction becomes blurred.

Each kind of organism must also have some way of getting about in the world, some means of dispersal. For most animals this implies some kind of locomotory behavior: flying, swimming, crawling, running. But locomotion is usually also involved in finding food, or in finding a sexual partner.

Growing up is universal and involves behavioral problems—like the unfolding of instinctive patterns, or the learning of ways of coping with the world. In thinking about this we quickly come to the fascinating problem of play, which seems to me undeservedly neglected by psychologists, perhaps in part because it is difficult to fit into any system, and in part because it is so hard to define. Puppies play, but do butterflies? And is professional football "play"?

There are various theories about the function of play. One common idea is that it serves as rehearsal for adult activity. This of course hardly explains adult play, except that adults may need to rehearse activities too. Another explanation is that play serves as a release for surplus energy—an idea that any human parent can understand. But play again may merge with both food and sex: a cat playing with a mouse, or children playing at sex.

When I talk about food and sex with psychologists, and wonder about other equivalent basic human drives, they almost always bring up aggression. I am beginning to wonder about psychologists, since they seem to see aggression everywhere. It is difficult to argue with them about it though, because if you disagree you are simply being hostile.

There is no denying the importance of aggression in human behavior—whether among psychologists or other people. Perhaps it is as basic and all-pervasive in man as food and sex; but I am not ready to admit it as a universal in animal behavior, comparable with nutrition and reproduction. It is a little hard, for instance, to imagine aggression among jellyfish. Animals often fight, all right, and the fighting, with associated states such as rage and fear, makes an interesting subject of study. The fancy psychological term for fighting is "agonistic behavior." But again there may be a blurring with nutrition and reproduction, since the fighting is often over food or mates.

I think it is easy to overestimate the importance of fighting in nature, partly because we ourselves are so much addicted to fighting that we tend to see it everywhere. We can visualize Tennyson's "nature red in tooth and claw" or Darwin's "struggle for existence" and we talk about our own "war" on insects or disease. It is harder to see the system of nature as something that is beautifully balanced, that has been working now for some hundreds of millions of years with organisms dependent on one another in an endless variety of ways. There are, on the one hand, competitive aspects of the system; and on the other, cooperative. Sometimes the cooperation is hard to see, though surely it is basic to the working of the system.

I like to make the remark that foxes are being kind to rabbits by eating them. Rabbit reproduction being what it is, the place would be overrun with them in no time if other animals were not using them for food—as was nicely demonstrated in the recent history of Australia. Rabbits, unchecked, would soon finish off the supply of low-growing plants on which they themselves feed, and soon would start to die of starvation. We are now finding a comparable situation with deer: since the "natural enemies" of deer have been so largely eliminated, hunting seasons and game limits have to be adjusted to keep the deer population within reasonable bounds.

Of course we need to distinguish between aggressive actions among individuals of different species and those among individuals of the same species. Rabbits and foxes are simply part of the complex web of exchange of food materials in the biological community. Fighting among rabbits themselves, or among foxes, would have quite different meaning. It is this point that interests us here, since we are trying to understand the curious human tendency to be mean to other members of the human species.

Fighting among individuals of the same species is common enough in nature, though far less noted than the hunt of predators for their food. In general, however, aggressive behavior within a species population in the wild rarely results in bodily harm. As Konrad Lorenz has pointed out in his delightful book on animal behavior, *King Solomon's Ring,* and in his later, more serious book, *On Aggression,* where teeth, horns or claws have developed to the extent that severe injury could be inflicted, some inhibition has developed concomitantly to govern the use of the weapons against other members of the same species. Thus fighting often takes on the character of stylized ritual, or of bluff.

Fighting among animals of the same species most often occurs over matters of territory, mates, food or resting places, and over social position in the case of animals that live in social groups.

The idea of territory is quite new in biology. It was first clearly stated in 1920 in a book by an Englishman, Eliot Howard, called *Territory in Bird Life.* Howard noticed that each pair of birds in his garden foraged over a rather limited area around the nest; when another bird of the same species attempted to intrude into the territory, it was driven off. In such fights the owner of the territory almost invariably won over the intruder. It now appears that an important function of bird song is the proclamation of territorial ownership, thus conserving the energy that would be wasted in fighting over the matter.

There is a large literature on territorial behavior. Such

behavior has been found to characterize many species of fishes, reptiles, birds and mammals, and similar behavior has been found among some insects and other invertebrates. Territory is now commonly defined as any area defended against intrusion by other individuals of the same species; thus defense, fighting, is basic to the idea. Among birds, depending on the species, the defended area may include mating, nesting and feeding areas, or mating and nesting areas but not the whole feeding ground, or nesting area only, or mating area only. The defended area may be the home of an individual, or a pair with young, or a large social group. Territorial behavior obviously serves to space individuals, reducing the danger of overcrowding; individuals that cannot establish territories because suitable areas are all occupied tend to be the first victims of predators.

One immediately begins to wonder to what extent territoriality explains some aspects of human behavior: the defense of the hearth, the home; of the fatherland; of the tribal area. Does our love of home and country, our suspicion of foreigners, have a deep-seated biological basis, or is it again something we have learned from our culture? Robert Ardrey thinks it is innate, and has developed the argument at some length in a recent book, *The Territorial Imperative*. There is no way of being sure without a time machine to go back and study the behavior of our prehuman ancestors; but we may be able to gain some insights by looking at living mammals, and especially at the behavior of our living primate relatives.

I have sometimes thought that the behavior of our prehuman ancestors may have been like that of the howler monkeys studied by C. R. Carpenter in Panama—which would be pretty much in accord with Ardrey's idea. Carpenter spent a year watching the monkeys every day on Barro, Colorado, an island nature reserve in Gatun Lake. He found that the howler monkey population of the island—a little less than 4000 acres in area—included about four hundred individuals divided among twenty-three clans, each occupying a definite territory. When clans happened to approach each other on the margins of their territories, the adult males set up a vigorous howling which continued until one group or the other retreated—howler monkeys have a very large larynx and are capable of making about the loudest noise in the animal kingdom. Carpenter never observed physical combat between the groups, though the howling was clearly unfriendly.

Maybe our ancestors also lived in small groups within clearly defined territories which they defended against intrusion by outsiders; and the defense may have taken the form of yells or the relatively harmless bluff of posturings. One can imagine that with the development of culture and tools the threat of yells might have given way to blows with clubs and stones—and the human animal would be started on his bloody career.

But gorillas and chimpanzees, man's closest relatives, show quite different behavior from that of the American monkeys. George Schaller, in his study of gorillas, found that each group had a definite area over which it ranged, but that there was a great deal of overlap among the areas occupied by different groups, with no attempt at defense of a single area by a particular group. Students call areas of this sort "home ranges" to distinguish them from defended territories.

Schaller was able to observe contact between groups on a number of occasions. Sometimes the groups, although quite close, would be seemingly oblivious of each other, and sometimes individuals from different groups would intermingle briefly without apparent hostility. In only one instance was there definite aggressive bluffing; this involved an encounter between the groups Schaller called "VII" and "XI."

Schaller's field notes for this incident read in part: "The silverbacked males of the two groups are only 20 feet from each other. The members of group VII sit clustered around their dominant male, but those of group XI are scattered. XI Dominant is greatly excited: he beats his chest, thumps the ground with one or both hands, emits a long series of hoots, and climbs a log only to jump with a crash into the vegetation below. He continues this for the next 1½ hours. VII Dominant, on the other hand, sits hunched over, his back to XI Dominant most of the time. Suddenly VII Dominant rises and walks rapidly toward the male of group XI. They stare at each other, their faces but one foot apart, for 20 to 30 seconds. Then VII Dominant returns to his seat . . . As XI Dominant beats his chest, VII Dominant rips off an herb, throws it into the air with an underhand motion and runs at the other male. They face each other silently with browridges nearly touching. They part. VII Dominant moves away and begins to feed."

Such is war among the ferocious gorillas. The charges of the males apparently always stop short of physical contact—whether the object of the attack is man, gorilla or other animal. And the brave chest-pounding and ground-thumping appear to be impressive bluff. These powerful animals, of course, are safe within their habitat except from hunting men and perhaps occasional leopards, so that they can afford to depend on bluff. For gorillas the chief form of aggression among themselves is staring—the animal that can stare the other down wins. In watching them Schaller himself had to be careful not to stare too intently, lest he provoke reaction.

Both howler monkeys and gorillas are vegetarian, whereas, as we have seen, the evidence indicates that animals in the human line have been predatory for a long time. This in itself makes it risky to look for the roots of human behavior in the actions of our contemporary pri-

mates. Social carnivores like wolves might be better models for study—but even among wolves there are behavioral
inhibitions which ordinarily prevent individuals of the
same species from inflicting serious damage on one another. How did man ever come to be such a violent creature, his own worst enemy?

However human meanness got started, we know that
it has characterized the hominid line for a long time. I
have already mentioned evidence of murder among the
Australopithecines and in Pekin man. So it is with a considerable proportion of all of the known hominid fossils:
over and over again fractures indicate that death was
caused by instruments in the hands of fellow-men.

Is it then "natural" for men to kill one another? Because people have been carrying on in this way for so long
in the past, does it mean that they will continue to do so
in the future? I suspect that the question of whether or
not war is natural is irrelevant. Disease, surely, is natural;
but this has not stopped us from trying, with considerable
success, to control it. The fact that efforts at controlling
war and murder in the past have always failed also seems
to me no argument against continuing to try—if we are
agreed that the objective is worthwhile.

Natural or not, the habit people have of killing one another is extraordinary when viewed in the perspective of
the biological community. I know of nothing comparable
among other kinds of animals—even the "wars" among
ants are between different species. The human phenomenon is so unusual that it should have some special name.
"Suicide" (self-killing) and "homicide" (man-killing)
come to mind, but they can hardly be used as general
terms because they already have particular meanings. In
a book published some years ago (*The Prevalence of People*) I proposed "anthropoktony," from the Greek *anthro-
pos,* man, and *ktonos,* to kill, as a general label for the

ave been weapons. These weapons
gned for hunting and for protection
out man started using them on his fel
ly date.

e innate basis, I am convinced that
tations of anthropoktony have varied
ons. One could hardly expect to find
hat would explain romantic suicide, arr
by torture for heretics, ritual blood sa
n war. Each variety of anthropoktony pr
rent explanation: the only common dend
imagination in developing ideas, and to
ng the ideas.

on to lethal meanness is as peculiar a ch
human species as is continuous sexual
and sex find similarly diverse expressio
suspect that man is the only animal that c
ds of habits he has developed. I have alrea
the loss of estrus may be due to the relax
rdinary rigors of natural selection, and th
y true of the proliferation of anthropokton
nal can afford to dedicate so much energy
ers of its own species; such behavior woul
pidly to extinction. But people keep on mu
dizzy rate despite their habit of killing on
iously, even the mass murders of modern wal
slowed the rate of population growth, pos
making up the losses rapidly.

the forms of lethal meanness are, they ar
pared with the variety of sublethal mean
eople have thought up. Maybe the psycholo
t about the universality of aggression among
even the meekest have a mean streak some

instructive to look briefly at these varieties
meanness, without going into any of the

phenomenon of people killing each other. It is an unwieldy word—but look at what it covers!

Anthropoktony is a specific kind of agonistic behavior. We might call it lethal meanness, as distinguished from the numerous forms of sublethal meanness practiced by humans. It is, however, far from a simple and unified phenomenon: people have developed endlessly diverse methods for killing one another, and they do it from a wide variety of motives. As far as methods are concerned, we have the simple brute force of strangulation; the use of hand tools such as knives and clubs; the development of tools that are effective at a distance, such as arrows and rifles; and finally the discovery of really wholesale ways of killing with the impersonal blasts of nuclear explosions. Death may be direct and immediate, as with a knife through the heart; or it may be inflicted surreptitiously by the use, for instance, of a slow-acting poison.

As for motives: one person may kill another simply out of bravado, to show he can, to add a notch to his gun or to bring home another head for the village collection of trophies. Or, as we noted in the last chapter, people may be killed for food: either as a staple article of diet, as a rare delicacy, as an emergency measure, or as a part of religious ritual. People are killed so that they may be robbed of their possessions; they are also killed from motives of hatred or revenge, or because in some way they form a real or imagined threat to the killers. Then there are the mass murders of war or massacre. Oddest of all, people are sometimes killed "for their own good." Occasionally it is proposed that people be killed for reasons of mercy, to end hopeless pain and misery—euthanasia. Usually, when people are killed for their own good, the killers are more appreciative of the benefits than the killed, as in the cases where heretics are burned so that their souls may be saved. Heretics, of course, are often killed not so much for their own good as for the good of society—to stamp out possibly contagious sin. Criminals likewise are supposedly executed for the good of society. Where they are imprisoned for their own good, for rehabilitation, we are dealing with a variety of sublethal meanness.

There are varying degrees of sociability in anthropoktony. The only solitary form is suicide: an individual killing himself because he can no longer face the problems of living. Suicide may be very public, as when a man lingers on the ledge of a tall building until a sizable audience has gathered. Sometimes the suicide is not only public, but carried out with a motive of public good, as in the case of the Buddhist monks who set fire to themselves in Viet Nam to publicize religious discrimination; or the case of the Kamikaze pilots of wartime Japan.

In instances where more than one individual is involved in the killing transaction, several grades of sociability may be usefully distinguished. First we have the situations in which only two people are involved: binary anthropoktony. The aggression here may be unilateral or reciprocal: the knife in the back versus the duel. Binary anthropoktony, to be sure, may occur incidentally in the course of complex operations, as in hand-to-hand combat during a battle, but this differs from the more usual types of murder because of the depersonalization of individuals among the conflicting masses. The classical combat between heroes is more like the simple binary pairing. Modern warfare would surely be both more picturesque and less messy if opposing field marshals or foreign ministers could be persuaded to engage in fencing matches instead of committing armies to battle.

Beyond the binary situation we get into numerical complexities: two to one, five to three, and so on. The important distinction however is not so much a matter of numbers as of social relations. I think we should distinguish between a "gang" and a "society" on the grounds that the

attitudes, motivation ⟨...⟩ may be quite different ⟨...⟩ Group meanness (or s⟨...⟩ the form of agonistic be⟨...⟩ an individual, as when ⟨...⟩ for some reason by his ⟨...⟩ an individual, as in the ⟨...⟩ gang, as with the street ⟨...⟩ outlaw gang; or of one so⟨...⟩

This looks neat enoug⟨...⟩ into the scheme—a com⟨...⟩ How, for instance, does ⟨...⟩ Negro in the southern Un⟨...⟩ society or by a gang? Per⟨...⟩ slot for mob actions since⟨...⟩ as contagious hysteria.

Contagious mass hysteri⟨...⟩ viduals, resulting in lynch⟨...⟩ may be directed toward a la⟨...⟩ sacre as a consequence. So⟨...⟩ think, "My, how bloody th⟨...⟩ be the British, Serbs, Mosle⟨...⟩ I stop to reflect though, I re⟨...⟩ to say that one society or o⟨...⟩ than another. All we Ameri⟨...⟩ our history of dealings wit⟨...⟩ course, don't necessarily inv⟨...⟩ mination of the Jews was del⟨...⟩ thought out.

What a dreadful record o⟨...⟩ underneath all of this blood⟨...⟩ some innate aggressive tende⟨...⟩ logical inhibitions by the d⟨...⟩ and ideas. Robert Ardrey, in ⟨...⟩ *sis*, suggested that man sho⟨...⟩ using animal" instead of the ⟨...⟩

tools seem to h⟨...⟩ presumably des⟨...⟩ beasts of prey; ⟨...⟩ at some very ear⟨...⟩

Whatever th⟨...⟩ present manife⟨...⟩ tural explanati⟨...⟩ single theory th⟨...⟩ robbery, death⟨...⟩ fice and moder⟨...⟩ ably has a diffe⟨...⟩ inator is man's⟨...⟩ for implementi⟨...⟩

The addictio⟨...⟩ acteristic of the⟨...⟩ —and murder ⟨...⟩ In both cases I⟨...⟩ afford the kin⟨...⟩ remarked tha⟨...⟩ tion of the o⟨...⟩ may be equall⟨...⟩ No other ani⟨...⟩ killing memb⟨...⟩ surely lead ra⟨...⟩ tiplying at a ⟨...⟩ another. Cur⟨...⟩ have hardly ⟨...⟩ war breeding⟨...⟩

Diverse as ⟨...⟩ nothing com⟨...⟩ nesses that p⟨...⟩ gists are righ⟨...⟩ people—that⟨...⟩ where.

It may be ⟨...⟩ of sublethal ⟨...⟩

subtleties of the psychology of aggression—I don't want to get entangled with ideas like sadism and masochism. Four main classes might be recognized: physical, verbal, vicarious and meanness to oneself, which I think could appropriately be called self-abuse. (There is nothing mean about self-abuse in its usual sense of masturbation, we are now told—one is enjoying oneself rather than abusing oneself.)

Physical versus verbal aggression gets us back to words again. Why can words hurt so? We all know at least a few people with very sharp tongues, people who can unerringly find a tender spot and hit home. But then again, I suppose all of us have been verbally hurt quite by accident, when there was no aggressive intent. In such cases I suppose our egos have been deflated in some way—what delicate egos we all have, even those who seem toughest.

Verbal aggression must go way back in human history: the curse, at least, has all the appearances of an ancient institution. Its history may well be mixed up with that of sympathetic magic, which "assume[s] that things act on each other at a distance through a secret sympathy" (to quote Sir James Frazer). As the doll in which pins are stuck represents the person one wants to injure, so the name in an incantation or curse is a symbol that can be manipulated for evil purposes. There are many societies in which personal names are kept secret because their owners fear that knowledge of their names would give enemies evil power.

The word can also stand as a symbol for the action, as when one man threatens to shit on the mother of another —a common Spanish insult. Mother is usually unavailable; it's the idea that hurts. But verbal and physical aggression blend together so that the distinction at times seems entirely arbitrary. Words can lead to blows easily enough, and two men fighting often mix insults with the physical combat.

Insults and fights are apt to be sudden aggression—flaring up and subsiding. There are also many forms of sustained aggression in which individuals or groups pick at one another for long periods of time or for life, as in the class or caste systems that seem always to develop in human societies. This is remarkably like the dominance hierarchy, or peck order, that has been observed in social mammals and birds; as with territoriality, one wonders whether there is some biological basis for the human behavior. But no other animal carries dominance and subordination to the extremes that people do.

To be sure, leadership or chieftainship doesn't necessarily involve meanness—though the idea of the benevolent dictator is somewhat self-contradictory. But as societies become complex and organized, overt meanness tends to develop. Even when a social system is institutionalized and completely accepted by all members of the society—even if the slave or serf or Southern Negro really likes "to know his proper place"—it seems to me that meanness is involved. And one can debate, of course, whether subordinate people ever like knowing their proper place.

The attitude toward slavery of those much-admired classical Greeks is curious. Certainly there were great thinkers among the Athenians, but the lot of the slave never engaged their sympathy. Reading Plato's *Republic,* or Aristotle's *Politics,* one can easily come to think what nasty people those Greeks were. Somehow they just could not see that the "slave mentality" they so despised was the product, not of the kind of people made into slaves, but of the system. As the great sociologist William Graham Sumner remarked in *Folkways,* "If any man, especially a merchant, who went on a journey incurred a great risk of slavery, why was not slavery a familiar danger of every man, and therefore a matter for pity and sympathy?" The woes of slavery were certainly pictured often enough in the tragedies, but the inequities of the system never worried the philosophers.

I suppose the explanation is that Greek economic life was completely dependent on slave labor and that philosophers are not apt even to notice the structure of their society, let alone to question it, unless some sort of breakdown has started. The first philosophers to question slavery were the Roman Stoics of the first century A.D.—Seneca, Plutarch, Pliny. By then the slave system of Rome had reached tremendous proportions, and the slave revolts underlined its miseries. According to Plutarch, Crassus crucified six thousand prisoners along the road from Capua to Rome after the defeat of Spartacus. This must have been quite a sight: enough to impress even a philosopher.

Slavery presumably started when people got the bright idea of keeping prisoners and putting them to work, instead of killing them. Sumner and other sociologists think that this may have been the origin of regular work habits: no man, they argue, would take up hard work unless he had to. But the example forced on the slaves gradually permeated other parts of society, and as slaves became scarce or disappeared other kinds of people began to work. Physical labor in the classical world was certainly regarded with scorn; the workman and the thinker, the artisan and the philosopher, lived in different worlds. One theory of the origin of modern science is that the failure of the slave supply in the Middle Ages forced the thinker to consider workaday problems—until, now, scientists combine the attributes of the artisan and the philosopher. One can argue that the modern workman is still a wage slave and that working conditions are often still far from ideal. Yet this, I think, is one of the areas in which mankind, at least within current Western civilization, has made real progress.

We like to think, in the United States, that we have established a classless society—and the Russians like to think the same thing about themselves. American sociologists, however, have spent a great deal of time studying our class system, and there is no doubt that class differences are real enough with us, and often very hard to transcend. In general though it seems to me that in parts of the Western world like the United States, Scandinavia, and some parts of the British Commonwealth, the classes are less mean to each other than in other parts of the world, or than at any prior time in the history of civilization. A Negro, a Jew, or a descendant of one of the recent immigrant groups might argue about this however.

We are getting into an area where aggression shades into discrimination, though I think discrimination should be classed as a kind of social, sublethal meanness. Here, along with racial, religious and national discrimination, we come across sexual discrimination—and perhaps we should also include age discrimination. Is the subordination of women a longstanding plot on the part of men, as Simone de Beauvoir, author of *The Second Sex,* seems to think? Certainly a great many women feel that they are victims of sublethal meanness on the part of men. They have made a long fight for voting rights, for education, for the right to earn a living and for equal pay; yet many occupations are still closed to them in the United States. Medical schools and law schools are apt to allow only a small quota of women to enroll, and female dentists in this country are extremely rare, though it is a common profession for women in some countries and dental technicians among us are mostly women.

We abuse our women, but we also abuse ourselves. I have often caught myself swearing at myself out loud after I have done something particularly stupid, though I rarely swear at other people. We are apt to call self-abuse disciplining ourselves, and this practice takes all sorts of forms. Fasting and celibacy are common kinds of self-denial in Western civilization, but we are capable of giving up almost anything that we like for our own good. Puritanism in general could be regarded as self-abuse, insofar as puritans live up to their own precepts.

Self-torture—hair shirts, flagellation and the like—have been epidemic at some times and in some cultures, but this behavior verges on the pathological forms of masochism and I don't want to get psychological.

But we all torture ourselves enough in the ordinary daily business of living, forcing ourselves to carry out all sorts of actions because we think we ought to. Whether this is good or bad I don't know; it seems to be unavoidable. We sometimes find an escape from the tensions and pressures, however, by taking a drink, or by following some other of the numerous shortcuts to happiness that mankind has discovered in the course of his cultural development.

VIII ❧ Shortcuts to Happiness

> "The desire to take medicine is perhaps the greatest feature which distinguishes man from animals."
>
> SIR WILLIAM OSLER, as quoted by
> ROBERT S. DE ROPP in *Drugs and the Mind*

OSLER, in the quote cited above, adds another item to the list of man's unique characteristics. Along with man's continuous sexuality, his addiction to internecine strife, his use of weapons, tools, symbols, fire, we have the human habit of resorting to medicine. Man the drug taker—*Homo medicans.*

A drug, in the widest and most proper sense, is any substance used in medicine. But it also has a narrow and special meaning to cover substances that are presumed to be habit-forming and harmful. We thus have drug as in drugstore, and drug as in drug addict, which is confusing. There is further confusion in that we seem to have no clear basis for determining which substances are drugs in the bad sense, except that they are substances socially disapproved of in our present culture. Cigarettes made from tobacco are currently not classified as a drug, but cigarettes made from marijuana are. Yet all of the evidence suggests that tobacco is both more habit-forming and more harmful to health than the product of the hemp plant. Marijuana, to be sure, has a more immediate dramatic effect than tobacco. In this respect it is comparable with alcohol; yet alcohol, whatever our attitude toward it, is not ordinarily thought to be a drug.

There is also a nice problem of distinguishing between materials taken to cure or alleviate some disease—medicines—and materials taken for kicks. Alcohol may be a valuable medicine in many situations, but it is not thought of as medicinal in the ordinary sense when taken at a cocktail party. And then there are all of the tranquilizers and stimulants that are prescribed by physicians as medicine, but have been taken up by the great American public as avidly as have cigarettes and alcohol. We have become a nation of pill takers, to the great benefit of the pharmaceutical companies. But there is now wide doubt about the benefit to our health.

I suppose we could well use the word "drug" to cover almost all materials taken for other than nutritional reasons. Or we could expand the meaning of "medicine" to include materials taken for ills of the spirit as well as ills of the flesh. Osler's dictum then becomes more meaningful. The variety of materials eaten, drunk, smoked, chewed, rubbed on the skin or otherwise used for nonnutritional purposes by different peoples is extraordinary. Every known culture has a system of medicine which includes the use of animal and plant products. Even the Australian aborigines, generally considered to have the simplest of technical cultures, have a considerable pharmacopoeia which includes such items as the inner bark of eucalyptus for congestion, pollen from bee nests for constipation, Mu-tir tree leaves for headache, and the like.

This dope-taking habit of man is so universal that it must have a long history, but since drugs rarely leave fossils we cannot be sure when the practice started, let alone how. When I try to think of anything comparable in other animals, I am driven back to the addiction of cats to catnip, or of sick puppies to eating grass, which are pretty feeble precedents. Maybe animals coming to salt licks would be a better parallel, except that the salt has nutritional value. I can recall nothing comparable with medicine-taking among wild primates.

My guess would be that the use of nonnutritional materials by man goes back at least to the time when fire was first tamed—and the use of drugs may initially have been purely magical, as I've indicated earlier I think was the case with fire. However he got started, primitive man in the long run did a very thorough job testing the animals and plants of his environment to find materials that were useful or that were thought to be so. And we are discovering that many items in the primitive pharmacopoeia really *were* useful. Civilized man hardly added anything to the list until the modern development of the chemical industry and of systematic testing of drugs on animals. Even now our debt to the past is tremendous. That most useful and mysterious of drugs, aspirin, derives from a prehistoric discovery of the effectiveness of willow bark in treating rheumatism. And, most recently, the whole array of tranquilizers comes from the discovery of the chemical nature of the juice of a plant, *Rauwolfia*, traditional in the pharmacopoeia of India.

I wonder again whether our ancestors tried out natural products so extensively that there is nothing left for modern science to discover. Or whether chemistry and medicine have become so insulated in the urban environment of the modern world that they are no longer inspired to continue the exploration of nature.

But my interest here is not so much in drugs taken as medicine to cure physical disease, as it is in drugs used as shortcuts to happiness—drugs that dull the hard edges of reality, or that produce excitement and heightened perception, or that lead the taker into a dream world where all is beauty and peace. These are the substances, in other words, that modify our mental state in ways that we find pleasurable or desirable. Curiously we have no general word for these substances. In our culture they are generally assumed to be bad—an aspect, I presume, of the same puritanical streak that makes sex dirty. The habit-forming and physiologically harmful drugs are sometimes classed as "narcotics." Although the dictionary defines a narcotic as a substance capable of producing "a deep unconsciousness," this is true of only some of them. And other so-called drugs are neither habit-forming nor demonstrably harmful. We need a word that will cover everything from opium to tea. The best I can do is to call them all pleasure-giving drugs—the drugs taken for kicks —though many of them, in their primitive context, were used seriously enough, being connected with religious or magical operations.

The list is a long one; and the substances that exist in nature were all discovered by our prehistoric ancestors. The great German toxicologist Louis Lewin classified them into five groups that are still most commonly used by pharmacologists. Lewin's groups are:

I. Euphorica: sedatives of mental activity, inducing in the person taking them a state of physical and mental comfort. Here belong opium and its components, morphia, codeine, etc., and cocaine.

II. Phantastica: hallucinating substances (we would now say "hallucinogens"). Here belong a number of vegetable products, differing greatly in chemical composition, which bring on visions, illusions and hallucinations, and may be accompanied or followed by unconsciousness or other symptoms of altered brain functioning. Examples are mescal buttons and Indian hemp (hashish, marijuana).

III. Inebriantia: the drugs of drunkenness. "A primary phase of cerebral excitation is followed by a state of depression which may eventually extend to complete temporary suppression of the functions." (I suppose that Lewin, by this last, means passing out.) The inebriating drugs include alcohol, chloroform, ether and benzine.

IV. Hypnotica: the sleep-producing agents or sedatives. Lewin lists chloral, veronal and sulphonal. Now we would add some of the barbiturates.

V. Excitantia: mental stimulants, now more commonly called analeptics. "Substances of vegetable origin which produce without alteration of consciousness a generally more or less apparent excitation of the brain." Here belong the plants containing caffeine, nicotine and the like: coffee, tea, tobacco, betel.

Nowadays we would add to this list a sixth group, the tranquilizers, or in medical jargon, the ataraxics. The ataraxics are not really new—they are just new to Western science. They stem from the discovery by Westerners in 1947 of *Sarpaganda,* a drug that had been used for many centuries in India by practitioners of a system of medicine known as the Ayur-Veda. Sarpaganda is the powdered root of a small bush, *Rauwolfia serpentina,* and it appears to have been regarded by the Ayur-Vedic physicians as an almost universal panacea for human troubles.

The story of the discovery of *Rauwolfia* by Westerners has been told by the American biochemist Robert S. de Ropp, in his book *Drugs and the Mind.* It started with the curiosity of the British biochemist Sir Robert Robinson and the enterprise of a Swiss pharmacologist, Dr. Emil Schittler, who persisted for five years in attempts to isolate the sedative substance of crude rauwolfia extracts— a white crystalline chemical which he named reserpine. Since 1952, when the discovery of reserpine was announced, a series of other ataraxics has been synthesized by ingenious chemists in various parts of the world and tested on troubled mankind. Spectacular results have been obtained with psychotics and neurotics—and also with ordinary people. Millions of Americans are now tranquilized—with what consequences no one can be sure, because the time has been too short for possible long-term effects to show up. Perhaps we have already reached Huxley's *Brave New World,* where life was made bearable by soma (a drug presumably akin to a traditional Indian medicinal beverage of the same name, derived from *Asclepias acida*).

The ataraxics are, for us at least, the newest of the shortcuts to happiness. The oldest, the most widespread and still by far the commonest of the chemical shortcuts is alcohol. That early man should have discovered alcohol is not surprising, since sugar-containing fruits ferment easily and quickly enough, especially in the tropics. One would only have to taste the fermenting fruit to discover the surprising and pleasant effects. The discovery that fermentation of grain can produce beer seems less obvious, as does cutting palm-flower stalks to get a sweet sap for palm wine—obtained from various palms in widely separated parts of the tropics. Most curious of all is the custom of chewing starchy materials so that they are mixed with saliva, and spitting the mixture into a bowl, where it rapidly ferments to make an alcoholic beverage. The saliva, of course, converts the starch into sugar. The chewing technique is practiced by such widely different peoples as South American Indians with Manihot, and Formosan tribes with rice. It is also the method used in preparing the nonalcoholic Pacific kava-kava. How did early man discover that something chewed and spat out would make a good drink? His concepts of disgust, obviously, were different from ours.

The use of alcoholic beverages is so widespread among peoples that the exceptions seem curious. The Australian aborigines had no fermented drink, the Indians of America north of Mexico apparently made very little use of alcohol before European contact, and alcoholic drinks were unknown in large areas of the Pacific. The case of the North American Indians is particularly puzzling because

they took to alcohol readily enough when they learned
about it from Europeans. The Indian tribes of tropical
America had a variety of ways of fermenting many different materials, and one would think that the agricultural
tribes of the north would have discovered the virtues of
fermentation. As for the Pacific, islanders almost everywhere now make toddy from the sap of the cut flower
stalks of coconut palms, but this is believed to be a modern
development.

Alcohol goes back as far as recorded history—and surely
much farther. Barley beer is mentioned in the oldest cu-
neiform writings of Mesopotamia, and some students consider it possible that grains were first cultivated for the
purpose of making beer. The Mesopotamians also had
wine made from dates and from sesame seeds, and they
imported some grape wine from vine-growing regions
(vines grew poorly in Mesopotamia because Dionysus had
cursed the area). The Egyptians had wine and beer, and
drunkenness seems to have been common. The first temperance tracts appear among the papyri. Wine is also frequently mentioned in the Bible, usually with approval:
"Give wine unto those that be of heavy heart." But the
Hebrews seem generally to have been a temperate people.
Among them, as is true of other ancient peoples, wine was
frequently mixed with water.

The knowledge of how to distill strong drink from the
weaker wines and beers is relatively modern. Credit for
the discovery is generally given to an Arabian alchemist,
Jabir ibn Hayyan, known to the West as Geber, who lived
in the eighth century A.D. The possibilities of distilled alcohol however were hardly realized until almost the end
of the thirteenth century, when Geber's writings reached
Arnaldus de Villanova, a professor of medicine at the University of Montpellier. Arnaldus, trying the distilling
technique, thought he had discovered the philosopher's
stone, the key to life everlasting. "Water of life" he called

it; and "aqua vitae," or "aquavit," it remains to this day for many people. Arnaldus' liquor, of course, was distilled wine: brandy.

The origin of other distilled liquors is obscure—though it is easy enough to see that once the source of the water of life had been discovered, people would try distilling anything they could ferment. The Dutch discovered gin, flavoring their clear aqua vitae with juniper—the Dutch *junever* or *jenever,* or the French *genevre,* or both, under English adaptation became first *geneva,* which was then quickly shortened. Whiskey probably orginated in Ireland; the word derives from the Irish-Gaelic equivalent of aqua vitae. The ascendancy of Scotland apparently dates from the discovery in 1860 by an Edinburghian named Andrew Usher that Highland malt whiskey and Lowland grain whiskey made a particularly satisfactory blend. The idea of distilling water of life from fermented molasses seems to have occurred first to the early European settlers in the West Indies, and rum became mixed up with the slave trade and with the early history of the American colonies. Bourbon, a purely American drink distilled from a mash of maize, did not become popular until after the American Revolution.

The human animal then has recognized the virtues of alcohol for a very long time. He has probably recognized its evils for almost as long, though in most ancient writings the strictures are against drunkenness rather than against drinking itself. The Chinese attitude, as stated in the *Shu Ching,* or *Canon of History,* about 650 B.C., sums this up nicely: "Men will not do without beer. To prohibit it and secure total abstinence from it is beyond the power even of sages. Here, therefore, we have warnings on the abuse of it."

Total prohibition was, however, tried by Mohammed. He acknowledged that wine had uses, "but the sin is more heinous than the usefulness." Devout Muslims have in general refrained from alcoholic drink, just as they abstain from eating pork. Yet there has also always been a pleasure-loving strain in the Muslim world—witness Omar Khayyám and his jug of wine, his loaf of bread and his boy. The bread was all right, but Mohammed was as much against loving boys as against loving wine—though neither prohibition seems to have been completely effective. Prohibition also has a long history in the Hindu tradition and is observed very strictly by some sects.

But attempts to control the drinking of alcoholic beverages have reached the greatest extremes in the legislation of English-speaking countries and Scandinavia. Finland and the United States both tried total legal prohibition, with equally dismal results. Liquor consumption in all of these countries is governed by complex legal regulations whose objectives are to mitigate the evils of drink. The situation in the United States, with federal, state and local controls, makes an especially confused pattern.

The temperance movement in the United States (curiously, "temperance" has always meant total abstinence in the language of the antialcoholics) got its organized start around 1840: a society called the Sons of Temperance, for instance, was formed in New York City in 1842, its members pledged never to touch the stuff. By 1850 the membership had reached 230,000, with lodges in most of the states east of the Mississippi (as well as several west of it), in four Canadian provinces and in England. The more famous Woman's Christian Temperance Union was organized in 1874 at Cleveland, with delegations from seventeen states. Temperance societies proliferated throughout the second half of the century, finally achieving effective coordination in the late 1890s through the Anti-saloon League of America. The movement gained political expression through the Prohibition party, founded in 1869, which has entered a candidate in presidential elections ever since. General John Bidwell ran most successfully, drawing 271,058 votes in 1892.

Maine prohibited the manufacture, distribution and sale of alcoholic beverages in 1846, and by 1855 thirteen states had similar laws, but except for Maine, New Hampshire and Vermont, the prohibition laws were short-lived. This was probably true in part because public interest was focused on problems of slavery and secession in the pre-Civil War period. In the 1880s a second wave of prohibitory legislation was initiated, but most of the states that then tried prohibition had repealed their laws by 1904.

The major wave of prohibition sentiment in America started in the decade before the First World War. By the time we entered the war in 1917, twenty-five states had prohibition laws of some sort. The drive against alcohol gained momentum during the war, culminating in the passage of the Eighteenth Amendment, prohibiting the manufacture, sale or transport of any intoxicating beverages; and the Congressional act named after Representative Andrew J. Volstead of Minnesota provided machinery for enforcement. The amendment, passed by Congress on December 18, 1917, was ratified by the necessary three-quarters of the states within thirteen months, and at 12:01 A.M. on Saturday, January 17, 1920, alcoholic beverages became legally prohibited for the entire United States—a magnificent victory for the so-called temperance workers. In the long run the Eighteenth Amendment was ratified by every state except Connecticut and Rhode Island.

Repeal, effective on December 5, 1933, was endorsed by a similarly large majority of the states. Why this complete turnabout in attitude on the part of a nation in the course of thirteen years? The failure of prohibition to prohibit, leading instead to the growth of a vast bootlegging industry outside the law, is well known. The preprohibition saloon keepers were not always constructive members

of society, but they looked pretty respectable compared
with their bootlegging successors. Alcohol became associated with all sorts of criminal acts, as are drugs today—
and one wonders whether the reasons are similar. But
while lawlessness was a powerful argument for repeal, it
may have been more of a symptom than a cause: surely if
a majority of the people had really wanted to continue
prohibition, they would have found some effective
method of law enforcement. The social reasons for the
failure of prohibition, like the reasons for its enactment
in the first place, were undoubtedly complex.

A detailed analysis of the prohibition movement would
be out of place here, but I cannot resist hauling in a few
ideas that I came across in the course of my reading.
Southerners tended to be in favor of prohibition because
it would help keep the Negroes in their place—alcohol
did not mix well with second-class citizenship. Industrial-
ists favored it because they associated labor agitation in
general with the conviviality of the saloon, but they found
that even without congenial saloon discussion people still
wanted better working conditions, shorter hours and more
pay. Beer was a German drink, an industry largely in the
hands of descendants of German immigrants—and remember the way everything German was anathema during the First World War; even Beethoven was suspect.

The sociologists point out that the truly upper classes
and lower classes have always liked to drink: the shift in
attitude toward alcohol is really a shift in the attitude of
the middle classes. The various temperance groups had
the support of the respectable elements in the community
—professional people, merchants, church leaders. Somehow during the period of prohibition social drinking infected the middle classes, and alcohol became more
respectable at the very time when it was illegal. Since the
repeal of prohibition, cocktail parties have become a
standard and perfectly proper form of entertainment in

suburbia. The temperance movement continues, with such organizations as the W.C.T.U. still very much alive, but the social basis of their support has changed.

As I write the only state still officially dry is Mississippi, which is curious because along the Gulf Coast, where the tourists flock, bars are wide open, without even making the pretense of being clubs. This supports the theory that prohibition in the South is largely an effort to "protect" Negroes from the evils of drink—the Mississippi law is no doubt effectively enforced in colored districts as far as open sale is concerned.

Prohibition has been repealed, but the feeling that there is something disreputable about alcohol is still with us. For instance, the word "saloon" has gone—never recovering from the slurs of the Anti-saloon League. We now have bars or taverns, cafés or cocktail lounges. We have achieved an extraordinary tangle of legislation governing the sale and consumption of alcohol. In some states you can drink anything at eighteen, in others only 3.2 beer; but in most states you must be twenty-one before you can legally buy an alcoholic drink of any sort. Laws about the sale of liquor on Sunday vary greatly, but in most localities the antiliquor bias of Protestantism makes it impossible to buy a drink until afternoon, when church services are over. There are laws about closing hours almost everywhere (New Orleans is one exception): midnight, 2:00 A.M., 4:00 A.M. In general drinks cannot be served on election days; and in the state of Washington they are prohibited on Arbor Day. Women may not approach a bar in Connecticut; and in Washington, D.C., you can buy only beer and wine at the bar—to drink hard liquor, you must sit at a table.

Thus we are still suspicious of alcohol, hedging it about with all sorts of restrictions. The other pleasure-giving drugs are all either completely prohibited or available only on medical prescription, except for Lewin's class of

Excitantia: tobacco and the pick-me-up drinks like coffee and tea.

Attitudes toward tobacco have gone through almost as many changes as have those toward alcohol. There have been sporadic legal prohibitions, and in many places at least it remains illegal to sell tobacco to minors, though the law is largely a dead letter. It is amusing to see cigarette machines in a college dormitory, where almost everyone is under twenty-one, with a sign saying that no minors are allowed to operate the machine. The Catholic Church at first tried to stop the spread of the tobacco habit, and it wasn't until 1725 that Benedict XIII, who liked to take snuff himself, rescinded the edicts against "dry drunkenness." Louis Lewin cites several countries, including Turkey, Persia and Russia, in which the death penalty was imposed for smoking. Smoking in the streets or other public places has often been prohibited, and it is still not customary to smoke in places of dignity like churches or law courts. Women who smoked in public in the United States before the First World War were not considered respectable.

About the bad effects of smoking there can be no doubt. The link between cigarette smoking and lung cancer seems clearly established; smoking is an important cause of chronic bronchitis, and there is evidence of a relationship between smoking and coronary heart disease. It is, all in all, a nasty habit and a great nuisance. Yet many haven't been able to break the habit, and the cigarette industry continues to flourish despite all health warnings. The use of tobacco is classed as "drug habituation" rather than "drug addiction" because it produces no demonstrable physical dependence on the drug or physiological withdrawal symptoms—the withdrawal symptoms are chiefly a nasty temper and an inability to think about anything except cigarettes. These symptoms can however be severe enough—as I know.

Tobacco may be chewed, taken as snuff, burned in a pipe, or the dried leaves may be rolled and burned by themselves as in a cigar, or with a wrapping of some other substance as in a cigarette. There are endless variations on each of these five basic techniques—particular tribes or regions have often developed their own peculiarities in the use of tobacco. But all five basic methods of use were discovered by the American Indians long before Columbus first dropped anchor off San Salvador and saw them indulging in the curious habit of drinking smoke from burning, rolled leaves. How on earth did the Indians discover all of these ways of getting a kick from the dried leaves of the tobacco plant?

But the mystery here is no greater than that surrounding man's discovery of other shortcuts to happiness. Take caffeine: in Asia, Africa and America early man discovered how to use several very different kinds of plants which have in common only the fact that they contain this drug. Coffee and kola are African; tea is Asiatic; while maté and guarana are American. Of these, only coffee and tea have conquered the modern Western world (unless Coca-Cola really depends on an extract of the kola nut for its appeal). Why these two have spread, while the others have not, is as mysterious as how they were all discovered in the first place. Maté is a tea-like drink commonly used over large parts of Brazil, Argentina and neighboring countries. It seems to me, at least, as pleasant and refreshing as coffee or tea; but all efforts to develop a wider market have failed, while coffee and tea support great industries and have become the mainstay of the economy of many tropical countries.

Coming out of the hills of Ethiopia somewhere around the year 1000, coffee conquered the Near East and then Europe with surprising speed. It has been said that if Mohammed had known about coffee, he probably would have prohibited it; but as it is, Muslims, forbidden to drink alcohol, are left with something that they can drink to provide a basis for conviviality and stimulation. The coffeehouse takes the place of the saloon. Coffee, to be sure, met some opposition, but nothing comparable with that against alcohol or tobacco.

Other pleasure-giving drugs listed by Lewin among the Excitantia are cocoa, betel and kava-kava. Cocoa (chocolate), another American discovery, contains small quantities of caffeine, but its principal drug, theobromine, is different, though related. Cocoa was the drink of the Aztecs and Mayas, but its great popularity in the outside world depends on the European discovery of the combination of cocoa (from Middle America) with sugar (from the sugar cane of India or the Pacific). One could argue now whether it should be classed as a drug or as a food—but theobromine, though weaker than caffeine, is definitely a stimulant.

The betel nut provides the chief stimulant for millions of people living close to the shores of the tropical Pacific and Indian oceans. The preparation of morsels for betel chewing is a somewhat complicated process, involving a piece of areca nut (the fruit of a palm tree, *Areca Catechu*), a fresh betel leaf, burnt lime, the leaf of another plant (*Piper betle*) and sometimes other materials. Methods for preparing the morsel vary from place to place, but once made up, it is chewed eagerly until nothing is left. Betel chewing, according to Lewin, arouses a greater craving in the addict than does any of the other Excitantia. "The greatest privations and sufferings of human life, insufficient or bad nourishment, hard work, rough weather, and illness lose their disagreeable character before the comforting action of the betel."

One wonders why this soothing morsel has not spread farther afield. Perhaps it is because the betel leaf must be fresh to be effective; or because various aspects of betel chewing are repugnant to the Western sense of good manners. Betel causes copious saliva flow, and we dislike spitting (except for those of us who chew tobacco) ; betel results in a bad breath; and it produces a bright red, bloody-looking mouth, which I find repulsive as well as startling. But for millions in the Pacific tropics it makes life bearable.

Kava-kava is another Pacific drug, used chiefly by the Melanesians (New Guineans, Fijians and the like) . The drink is based on the fibrous root of a plant, *Piper methysticum,* which is thoroughly chewed, usually by the young men and boys with strong teeth; the masticated product is spat into a bowl and diluted with water for drinking. There is no fermentation, so the process is quite different from that of chewing starchy roots to make alcohol: the active principle is a resinous substance which Lewin named *yangonin.* This drug induces a euphoric state, "refreshes the fatigued body and brightens and sharpens the intellectual faculties" (to quote Lewin) . "Kava has a soothing effect. Those who drink it are never choleric, angry, aggressive and noisy, as in the case of alcohol."

It sounds like a pleasant and innocuous shortcut to happiness, but it was bitterly denounced by the missionaries, who succeeded in abolishing the use of kava on many of the islands. It seems to have been largely a social and ceremonial drink: served when entertaining guests, when discussing public affairs, when negotiating with other tribes, when celebrating some event like the planting of trees or the building of houses. Europeans have tried to prepare it by substituting grinding and mashing for the chewing process, but the end product is said to be inferior to the kava drink prepared in the traditional manner.

I have written a chapter on drugs and hardly mentioned the products of hemp, of poppy, or of the coca tree, nor any of the odd products that various peoples have used to find illusion, heightened perception or peace of mind. There remains always the puzzling problem of how our ancestors discovered these pleasure-giving drugs; and the problem, still with us, of whether they are good or bad; whether they should be prohibited by society, controlled or freely indulged in. It is clear that we cannot look at these drugs without prejudice, and that our attitudes are as much a consequence of our culture as of the properties of the drugs themselves. But that is the subject of another book, and several such books have been written.

To me the last word in drug taking is the custom many peoples of Siberia have—of using a dried mushroom, the fly agaric (*Amanita muscaria*), as a way of finding some pleasure through the long, dark winters of their homelands. They obtain the agaric with difficulty by trading with peoples who live farther south, where the mushroom grows. But fortunately they can make a little go a long way, because the active principle of the agaric is excreted in the urine: so, by pissing in a common pot and continuing to drink the accumulation, they can prolong their orgy for days. Obviously they must have very different ideas from those that govern our behavior, not only about what is disgusting, but also about what is proper and decent. But where did we get our ideas about decency, propriety and respectability?

IX ❧ The Pursuit of Gentility

"By *genteelism* is here to be understood the substituting, for the ordinary natural word that first suggests itself to the mind, of a synonym that is thought to be less soiled by the lips of the common herd, less familiar, less plebeian, less vulgar, less improper, less apt to come unhandsomely betwixt the wind and our nobility."

H. W. FOWLER,
A Dictionary of Modern English Usage

MY MOTHER was a very proper person. For her all words, things, acts—and people—fell into one or the other of two categories: they were either nice or not nice. Some acts that were not nice, like urination and defecation, unfortunately were necessary, but at least they could be delicately hidden under cover of meaningless words. I was taught, for instance, to refer to piss as "number one" and to shit as "number two." These words, of course, instead of remaining meaningless, acquired all of the associations and connotations of the respective physiological functions; they became "dirty words" for me. I still remember my shock at an early age when I heard a grocer refer to a grade of potatoes as "number two." One simply did not use such a phrase in public, for something to be eaten!

Mother's attitude has left me in a sort of general rebellion against niceness—at least I think that's the explanation. At any rate it now seems to me absurd to hear a child ask his mother if he can go "tinkle" in the bathroom. And the label "rest room" always brings to mind a *New Yorker* cartoon of many years ago of a car parked at a filling station, captioned with the mother's comment to an impatient child, "Daddy was very tired, dear." I resolved to cut this nonsense and bring up my own children on Anglo-Saxon monosyllables—an idea that did not get enthusiastic support from my wife for some inexplicable reason.

The situation with our daughters was somewhat confused because they were all born abroad, with Spanish serving as their primary language; and anyway our arrangement early in marriage was that Nancy would have responsibility for the education of daughters, and I for sons. Because my son Glenn was born in the United States and his primary language was English, I had a chance to test my ideas.

For a while everything went along smoothly. His nurse Junie was a young lady of Scottish descent from Nova Scotia—a strikingly beautiful blonde. I am sure her vocabulary with Glenn was quite different from mine; but she was at least tolerant of the eccentricities of the family she worked for. There were limits however.

We were living in Greenwich, Connecticut—a reasonably proper town, at least on the surface. One day Junie came home with Glenn, furious. They had gone downtown and come back on a crowded bus. At some quiet moment Glenn had called out in his clear, childish voice—"Junie, I farted!"

I was told, in no uncertain terms, that this had to stop. Gentility—niceness—had won another battle. I gave up —for a couple of years. When I resumed vocabulary building I hoped that the children had learned discretion, had learned that our culture demands double-talk. Or perhaps I should say that our society demands the adaptation of vocabulary to circumstances. My wife was never sure about Glenn's discretion (I wasn't either) and we could sometimes imagine the reactions of horrified schoolteachers, but no further incidents came to our attention.

I still don't see why words for bodily functions are better if they are derived from Latin or Greek roots. I don't understand the psychology of euphemisms—except that it is somehow related to word magic, to the confusion of words with the things they stand for. In this respect verbal indecency is like verbal aggression: the symbol has acquired a force similar to that of the act.

We are gradually becoming more relaxed about words, both in talking and in printing, though we still have a long way to go before anyone can say we are being natural —at least in the case of those proper American middle classes. The vocabulary of men in the army or navy seems natural enough, though I am not sure how they talk with their girl friends or wives. Even the middle classes are becoming more tolerant toward what they read, though their talk is still pretty inhibited—nice. I have never had the courage to use a taboo word in a public lecture, even when it seemed the most apt and appropriate expression —but look at what I have been writing.

The relaxation of the taboo on words in print started in 1933 with the judgment of Judge John Woolsey in the case of James Joyce's *Ulysses*, delivered in the United States District Court for the Southern District of New York and subsequently upheld by the New York Circuit Court of Appeals. Judge Woolsey's lucid and closely reasoned opinion has been printed as a foreword in all Random House editions of the book, and thus has presumably been read by some hundreds of thousands of people. *Ulysses* previously had been banned by United States Customs as obscene because of dirty words in the text. But to quote the judge, "The words which are criticized as dirty are old Saxon words known to almost all men, and, I venture, to many women, and are such words as would be naturally and habitually used, I believe, by the types of folk whose life, physical and mental, Joyce is seeking to describe." Given Joyce's intent, avoidance of these words would have been, the judge noted, "artistically inexcusable."

The decision on *Ulysses* did not mean that the ban on taboo words had been lifted: it was simply one step in the relaxation process. The next major step, I think, was the publication by Scribner's in 1951 of James Jones's *From Here to Eternity*. "Fuck" and "shit" here came out into the open with some frequency in straightforward, easily readable dialogue. I have been told that the editors tried at first to cut the Jones vocabulary, but that this obviously damaged the realism of the dialogue. The forbidden words were put back in considerable numbers, enough at least to restore Jones's intent to give the feel of soldier language. I suspect that this was done with considerable trepidation on the part of the publishers. I understand that they went over the proofs with legal advice, carefully counting the number of times that each taboo word was used. They must still have had reservations about the extent to which the book could be realistic. Cocksucker, for instance, does not occur in the book, though it is a common enough item in soldier talk.

I have heard Jones say that he would not have been able to write *From Here to Eternity* as he did without the precedent of Norman Mailer's *The Naked and the Dead*, where the effect of the meaningless and monotonous "fucking" of soldier talk is achieved by the substitution of "fuggin." Mailer in turn surely owes a debt to Hemingway, and so one could go on, tracing the history of openly published realistic dialogue backward from *From Here to Eternity* or forward to such more recent books as John Rechy's *City of Night*.

Relaxation of taboo has been slower in books of nonfiction than in novels, which in some ways is curious, since one might think that freedom from cultural restrictions would come first in scholarly books—except that scholars are notably timid. As I write this there has been considerable fuss about a book by Wayland Young called *Eros Denied,* in which he writes "fuck" when he means "fuck" instead of using "copulate" or "mate" or "have intercourse" or any of the other awkward substitutes for the natural word. "Fuck" is still not in Webster's Third New International Dictionary, though "shit" made it this time. The freest use of taboo words that I have seen yet is in an amusing little book by Edward Sagarin called *The Anatomy of Dirty Words,* published in 1962. I have not noticed any furor over this book, perhaps because it has not come to the attention of a very large public. (I discovered it through a book review in a learned journal, *The American Anthropologist.*) On the other hand, Oscar Lewis' *La Vida,* a work of anthropology that freely and matter-of-factly records the vivid language and sexual habits of its subjects, has been widely reviewed, without anyone seeming shocked by the language or the sexual details. But the problematic words and incidents have not been quoted in the reviews.

Taboo words still do not appear in scholarly journals. One could argue that this is understandable because of the scholarly tendency to use the longest word whenever there is a choice, so that "having intercourse" would seem more appropriate than "fucking," just as "prostitute" would be used instead of "whore," even though there is no strong taboo on the latter. But in reporting interviews, too many psychologists and anthropologists still delicately hide behind asterisks or circumlocution, though surely no unformed young mind is ever likely to read their words. In clinical psychology the avoidance of the words actually used by the patient may even be misleading, since we then have, not what the patient said, but only the psychologist's interpretation of what he meant. Very likely this avoidance is in part a concession to the Post Office, which keeps a sharp eye on journals, magazines and newspapers that go through the mails. And officials of the Post Office Department appear to be very easily shocked by events in the world around them.

This leads to the general problem of obscenity, pornography and censorship. "Obscene," according to my faithful friend the Oxford English Dictionary, comes from the Latin *obscenus,* meaning "repulsive, filthy, disgusting," though the etymology is admittedly doubtful. "Pornography" comes directly from the Greek and means "writing about harlots." If the original meaning of obscenity is filth, it is a sad commentary on our minds that it has come to cover direct reference to sexual activity. I am reminded of an article in the *New Statesman* of July 24, 1964, on topless dresses. According to the author, the prosecuting counsel in a case in California accused a very pretty young woman who had exposed her breasts of "throwing filth in the faces of the police and the public." As the author of the article goes on to say, "If breasts are repulsive, filthy or loathsome, why are we invited to admire the Venus de Milo? Surely the answer is precisely the opposite: a woman's breasts, far from being repulsive, filthy and loathsome, are, or can be, attractive, beautiful and desirable. The obscenity, if any exists, must and can only lie in the eyes and mind of the beholder. What the law is in fact saying is that women must not expose their breasts because *men* are obscene."

Preoccupation with obscenity, in the sense of regarding sexual organs and sexual acts as filthy, seems to be a peculiar characteristic of modern Western civilization, finding particularly strong expression in the English-speaking countries. The first notable case of a publisher or bookseller being convicted for "obscene libel" in Britain was that of Edmund Curll, in 1727. Curll published frankly pornographic books and pamphlets for some forty years, quite profitably and without serious trouble with the law.

His difficulty came with a book called *Venus in the Cloister*, which purported to describe sexual activities in certain French convents, so that religious feelings as well as sex were involved. Even this might not have cost him much trouble, except that while out on bail he published a book of "scandalous and seditious" political recollections called *The Memoirs of John Ker*. He was fined on both the obscene libel and political charges, but the political indiscretion was probably taken more seriously than the obscenity. The prosecutor for the Crown had no specific law against obscenity to invoke, but he maintained that Curll had committed a common law misdemeanor: "What I insist upon is that this is an offence at common law as it tends to corrupt the morals of the King's subjects and is against the peace of the King."

Anti-vice feelings continued to grow in England after the Curll episode. In 1787, King George III issued a proclamation asking his subjects to "suppress all loose and licentious prints, books and publications, dispensing poison to the minds of the young and unwary, and to punish the publishers and vendors thereof." The Society for the Suppression of Vice was founded in 1802 and started on the long job of cleaning up British morals. By 1857 the Vice Society was responsible for 159 prosecutions, of which only five resulted in acquittal. The prosecutions were for out-and-out pornography, the "filthy picture" sort of trade with no pretense to literary or artistic merit. But despite this effort, pornography continued to flourish, its products sold fairly openly on the streets of London.

In 1857, Parliament passed the Obscene Publications Act, largely as a consequence of the efforts of Lord Campbell, Chief Justice of the Queen's Bench and later Lord Chancellor. This act empowered magistrates to order the destruction of prints and books if, in their opinion, publication would amount to a "misdemeanour proper to be prosecuted as such." The ordinary English magistrate was thus turned into a censor of literary and artistic morals. The bill met with considerable opposition in both Houses—many members did not think much of attempts to make people virtuous by Act of Parliament—but it passed, though much amended.

In the United States, governmental preoccupation with the protection of citizens from obscenity also started early in the nineteenth century. The first law against obscenity was passed in Vermont in 1821, the second in Connecticut in 1834, with Massachusetts following a year later. In 1842, Congress included in the Customs Law a prohibition of the importation from abroad of obscene materials; but attempts to get Congress to prohibit interstate traffic in obscenity failed. In the first part of the nineteenth century Congress was still sensitive to the idea that all mail must be carried: that the monopoly on delivery did not include the power of censorship of contents. In 1835 a law designed to prohibit material likely to incite Southern slaves to rebellion failed to pass, being opposed by both Southern and Northern senators on grounds of constitutionality, though surely slave rebellion was a more serious danger than sexual corruption.

The most prominent figure in the crusade against pornography in the United States was Anthony Comstock. He was instrumental in forming the Committee for the Suppression of Vice in New York in 1872, and it was largely as a result of his personal efforts that Congress passed, in 1873, the basic law prohibiting obscenity in the mails that, with trifling changes, still governs Post Office policy. Comstock was made a special agent of the Post Office and given police power; he bragged that within the first year he had seized and destroyed 194,000 obscene pictures and photographs and 134,000 pounds of books. In 1905, Comstock tackled the theater, using as his target the new play by that "Irish smut-dealer" George Bernard Shaw, *Mrs. Warren's Profession*. The attack failed (by a vote of 2 to 1 in a three-man court) , but it led Shaw to add the word "comstockery" to our vocabulary, with the meaning of "ludicrous prudery."

The attempt to prohibit pornography—writing or art designed to provoke sexual arousal—is thus relatively new. There were no such laws in the classical world—how could there be when Priapus was a god? In ancient Greece plates and drinking bowls for children were decorated with representations of sexual intercourse, to give the kids something amusing to look at. The antisex bias of our culture is usually blamed on the Christian tradition, and especially on the influence of Saint Paul—though goodness knows there is plenty of sex in the Bible, including, it can be maintained, plain pornography.

Whatever action was taken against pornography in the early days of Christianity would have been by the church and not the state—a matter of canon rather than civil law. The church however seems not to have taken much interest in the matter until the time of the Reformation. The *Index* of prohibited books was instituted in 1564; even then, the church seems to have been more worried about heresy and satire that tended to ridicule or undermine authority than about obscenity.

Why then did pornography become a major issue in British and American law after 1800? The usual explanation is that worries about obscenity coincided with the spread of education. As long as only the elite could read, no one was concerned about the effect of reading on their morals; but the common people had to be protected.

Drs. Eberhard and Phyllis Kronhausen, in their book *Pornography and the Law*, distinguish hard-core pornography, erotic realism and erotic humor. Hard-core pornography is written expressly to arouse sexual feelings. The dark aspects of sex—disease, unwanted pregnancy, tawdry settings, hurts and despair—are not mentioned. The realistic writer, on the other hand, tries to picture life as it is,

which certainly always includes sexual reactions, sometimes involving great pleasure and sometimes great pain.
As for humor, sex often gets people into situations that, to
others at least, seem funny; it is a notable subject for jokes,
and its humorous aspects have attracted a number of great
writers, from Rabelais to Mark Twain—and remember
such classical authors as Aristophanes.

Except for psychopathic crusaders like Anthony Comstock, to whom all sex is anathema, hard-core pornography has been the main object of legal and social attack,
chiefly on the grounds that it corrupts the mind and leads
to antisocial behavior. Whether this is really true or not
no one seems to know, though a great many people have
very strong opinions. In reading and thinking about this
I have come to agree with the numerous psychologists
who believe that pornography does not have antisocial
effects. Robert Lindner (as quoted in the Kronhausens'
book) has stated this position well:

"As a psychoanalyst who has had more than a decade of
experience with the emotionally disturbed, and especially
with delinquents, I am convinced of the absurdity of the
idea that any form of reading matter, including so-called
comics and 'other objectionable books,' can either provoke
delinquent or criminal behavior or instruct toward such
ends . . . I am convinced that were all so-called objectionable books and like material to disappear from the
face of the earth tomorrow this would in no way affect the
statistics of crime, delinquency, amoral and anti-social
behavior, or personal illness and distress."

It seems to me that reading, instead of leading to antisocial behavior, is more likely to serve as a harmless release for impulses that otherwise might provoke such behavior. Pornography, if this is true, would represent vicarious sexual activity—a point made by the Kronhausens.

Beyond obscenity and pornography we have the problem of vulgarity—a matter of social custom rather than of law or rule. Vulgarity contrasts with respectability, gentility and elegance. Preoccupation with being genteel and respectable reached the height of absurdity in Victorian England, coinciding with the development of the anti-vice crusades. But respectability, like vice, is still with us; and our present problems with standards of respectability and rebellion against them can be looked at as a legacy of the last century. One can, of course, look back over the history of Western moral attitudes, as several authors have, and find continually shifting patterns of repression and indulgence. Though, of course, the whole past goes into the building of our heritage, we are the direct descendants not so much of the Elizabethans, or even the Puritans, as of the Victorians.

Sir Harold Nicolson in his amusing and instructive survey of *Good Behavior* has attempted to trace the sources of nineteenth-century British respectability. He thinks that the chief cause lay in the rapid expansion of the middle and lower-middle classes with the development of industry and trade. "Instead of taking for granted the station into which they had been born," he writes, "men and women began to be self-conscious about it and competitive . . . Everybody wished to rise into the category above them, or at least to differentiate themselves by shibboleths, possessions and pretences from the category believed to be immediately below." Hence the cult of finely graded gentility so beautifully portrayed in the novels of Jane Austen. In *Sense and Sensibility* Miss Austen remarks of the two Miss Steeles: "Lucy was certainly not elegant and her sister not even genteel." Sir Harold notes, "It caused pain to her heroines if these minute distinctions were either not recognised or regarded as immaterial. It shocked Emma to realise that Mr. Elton, while 'so well understanding the gradations of rank below him,' should fail to observe that she herself was his social superior 'both in connection and mind.' "

It is customary to attribute the snobbishness of Miss Austen's characters to her fine sense of humor and her genius for irony. But Sir Harold remarks that "her published correspondence leaves behind it an uneasy suspicion that she was not always intent on caricaturing the vulgarity of others: that sometimes she reveals her own."

Miss Austen's characters, of course, scorned trade, but they did like money; and the money, in the long run, came from trade and industry. Sir Harold's economic explanation thus makes sense. But along with this he gives about equal weight to a religious trend: the influence of John Wesley and his followers, and later, the Oxford Movement within the Established Church. In the United States, Methodism spread greatly during the nineteenth century and was surely related to the spread of narrowly restrictive attitudes toward conduct and language. But it is difficult to see Methodism as a cause of the spread of the cult of gentility; to me it looks like another symptom. The Puritan tradition has always been strong in the United States, infecting almost all of the numerous Christian denominations. I have to say "almost all" because of Unitarians and perhaps some shades of Episcopalians. But even these, if not puritanical, at least have managed to be eminently respectable.

In addition to the economic and evangelic explanations of the cult of respectability, Sir Harold cites as secondary causes "a morbid preoccupation with the sense of shame" and a "profound moral reaction occasioned by the excesses of the French Revolution." About the prevalence of a sense of shame in the nineteenth century there can be no doubt; it is still very much with us. And the shame about bodies, about sex, and about excretory functions is certainly a large component of Victorian gentility. But what led to this overdevelopment of the sense of shame as compared with attitudes in the preceding centuries, and attitudes that are slowly coming to prevail now? I don't know, and I have not come across any explanation that appeals to me as reasonable. I don't think Sir Harold is right in treating shame as a contributing cause of the cult of respectability; more likely it is simply another manifestation of that cult.

I do think, however, that Sir Harold is quite right about the importance of the British reaction to the French Revolution. The revolutionaries were obviously a bunch of dirty atheists, and their undermining of property, status and long-established custom were all part and parcel of this irreligious attitude. The French were just across the Channel, and people with any stake in the British social system were both horrified and scared. Even such obviously beneficial consequences of the Revolution as the metric system of measurement failed to make any impression in Great Britain—meters and grams were not nice.

Of course the metric system also failed to penetrate the United States, but I think this was chiefly because we were too lazy to change. The French Revolution was far away and our own Revolution too close for us to share the British horror. But I think we can sense the British reaction in the last century by looking at our present reaction to Russia. The words "communist" and "atheist" have become closely associated, so that we are sometimes urged to fight the communist menace by joining some church and supporting daily prayers in the public schools—however irrelevant this may seem. But it does help us see the force added to the British evangelical movement by the excesses of the French Revolution.

I have gone somehow from obscenity to respectability, and being respectable in the Victorian sense involves a great deal more than avoiding obscenity. What does it involve, anyway? In search of help I turned to the Oxford

English Dictionary. The fourth meaning of respectable, I found, is "Of good or fair social standing and having the moral properties naturally appropriate to this. Hence, in later use, honest or decent in character or conduct, without reference to social position, or in spite of being in humble circumstances." This part of the dictionary was published in 1908, so it appears that moral qualities at that time still seemed "naturally appropriate" to social status. This was in England, of course, but I suspect the American middle classes had similar ideas.

Respectability—and gentility—then, are deeply involved with the idea of social class. And social class, as I remarked in the discussion of sublethal meanness, is still very much with us. I do think though that we are making progress toward the equality of opportunity envisioned by those Founding Fathers. As one sign, I find no mention of social status in the definitions of "respectable" in Webster's Third New International Dictionary, which was published in 1961. Status may still be involved, but at least the editors of this dictionary didn't think so.

I have been trying to analyze the cause of my dislike of the idea of respectability. Perhaps because respectability is so often fraudulent: the properly dressed, properly spoken, properly mannered gentleman may be a complete knave, while the laborer wearing blue jeans and using obscenities may really be a good guy. We do tend to judge people by their appearances. I suppose there isn't much else to go by in the case of casual encounters, but the system often fails and often involves hurts. I am not arguing for uniformity—far from it. But I would like to see our diversity built on some system that would entail a minimum of hurts—and that would allow true equality of opportunity.

I suppose that the opposite of respectable, as I am using the word, is vulgar. The idea of vulgarity, I suspect, was an invention of the middle classes to keep the lower orders in their places—or at least to give the genteel something to feel smug about. Vulgarity shows up easily in language. Endlessly reiterated and meaningless obscenities, for instance, are used more freely by the average soldier or sailor than by the officer; by the average workman, than by the executive. The argument works both ways, of course, since the vulgar may take pride in their identification through vulgar usage. I have sat in on discussions among enlisted men about whether it was possible to be an officer and not be a bastard. Since I have never been directly involved as a member of the armed forces, I have no opinion based on experience. But I do think that the middle classes, while they may get pleasure out of being smug, miss a lot in life—and not only because of restrictions on vocabulary.

Discussion of vulgarity rapidly leads to general questions of manners and etiquette. Manners, I suppose, covers the way people actually and habitually behave toward one another, whether "good" or "bad"; etiquette covers the formal rules for behavior, often carefully spelled out, and in situations like court etiquette, rigidly enforced. Good manners and proper etiquette vary tremendously from one cultural situation to another, and are often the cause of misunderstandings—and sometimes of amusement.

People communicate through gestures and attitudes as well as words, as the anthropologist Edward Hall has so nicely demonstrated in his book *The Silent Language*. Gestures are as universal as words in interpersonal relations and might well be considered more basic, more "natural" than articulated speech—baby smiling or crying, for instance. Sign languages may work not only within a species but between species—the tail wagging of dogs, for example, and the snarling or growling of many animals as signs of anger. In view of this, it is curious that we do not find more uniformity in the use of gestures among different peoples. Yet these vary not only with cultures, but with social class.

The extended hand, or the handshake, is about as universally understood as any gesture; yet whether to shake hands can become very complicated. A man isn't supposed to extend his hand to a lady, as I remember; though in our culture, if a woman extends her hand, the man should take it; Continentals, at least of the courtly type, would kiss it. The British in general are not much given to handshaking—something to do with their well-known reserve. Americans who like to think they are upper class would tend in this, as in other things, to imitate the British, avoiding the "glad hand" and the "pleased to meet you" of the vulgar. Latins, on the other hand, tend to shake hands on every possible occasion; and in some countries and some social situations at least, they go even further with a stylized embrace. All of this without reference to the personal variations from the hearty and even painful grasp to the limply extended hand.

The complications of handshakes, however, are nothing compared with the complex problems of who kisses whom, where, and how. Complex kissing manners seem to be primarily a characteristic of Western civilization, but with deep historical roots in classical cultures, including the Hebrew. This is particularly true if we define "kiss" as contact with the lips—either lip with lip, or lip with some other part of the body. Other gestures, like nose rubbing, may play similar roles in other cultures where lip contact would be regarded as abhorrent.

The Romans had three different words for the three basic varieties of the kiss: *osculum* was the kiss of greeting between friends on face or lips; *basium* the kiss of affection, lips to lips; and *suavium* the "deep kiss" of lovers. We still have the distinctions, though no modern language echoes the Latin vocabulary fully: perhaps this indicates that kissing was even more important in the ancient world than in the modern. Certainly in the Graeco-Roman world kissing was common in ceremonial and religious acts; as a salutation among friends; as a sign of family affection; and as a seal of love.

That religious kissing antedates Christianity is shown by Cicero's complaint that the lips and beard of the statue of Hercules at Agrigentum were almost worn away by the kisses of the devout. Kissing was taken up with enthusiasm by the early Christians, who used it as a symbol of fellowship, following the injunction of Saint Paul: "Salute one another with a holy kiss." This may have contributed to the widespread ancient belief that the early Christians were immoral as well as obnoxious. At any rate Tertullian mentions that it was later ordered that men should salute only men, and women, women, in this way. But the practice of kissing holy objects has persisted.

Kissing as a form of greeting has dropped out among men, at least in the Anglo-American world; but in the middle-class United States it is still all right for men to greet women they know fairly well with a kiss on the cheek. I've never been quite sure which women among my friends should be treated this way, but it seems to be a good rule, when in doubt, to try it, since it is taken as a sign of affection and warm approval. Women, at least at times, greet each other with a kiss and an embrace: my wife tells me that this is most usual when they haven't seen each other for a long time, or when there is some special need for comfort.

Within the family, fathers stop kissing their sons at a fairly early age—the exact age depending on the degree of demonstrativeness characteristic of the family. Fathers can continue giving their daughters a ceremonial cheek kiss indefinitely, as mothers can kiss both daughters and sons. The question of what relatives are kissed outside the nuclear family is more complicated: there is probably some regional variation as well as difference according to social class; and certainly individual families differ considerably in kissing practices as well as in other manifestations of cohesiveness. Mouth-to-mouth kissing however is very generally taboo except among actual or potential sexual partners. In the United States at least, we have moved a long way from Victorian gentility, when mouth kissing was almost as intimate an act as sex itself. Undergraduates nowadays are extremely uninhibited.

The kissing problem is similar to the first-name problem in many ways. Again the Victorian practice was very restrictive: married couples might continue to refer to each other as Mr. and Mrs. in public—and perhaps even in private. Now, at least among undergraduates, last names have practically disappeared: from first meeting, people call each other Bill or Mary or George, and sometimes don't even know the last names of their friends.

The problem of when to use first names in the United States is similar to the problem of when to use the familiar form, when to *tutoyer*, in languages other than English. If I can judge from the few people with whom I use *du* in German, the decision in that language is still formal: two people decide that they know each other well enough to use the familiar form, drink *Brüderschaft,* and speak in the second person from then on. In my experience the decision to use *tu* in French is similarly a matter of mutual agreement. In both languages one reaches a first-name basis some time before reaching the degree of familiarity implied by the second-person pronoun.

Usage in Spanish varies greatly in different countries, and I suppose in different social circles. Colombia is extremely formal: children even address their parents with *Usted.* If I use the first name with anyone, I believe he should use mine, and this applies also to the familiar pronoun form. But in all the years I lived in Colombia I never was able to persuade the laboratory staff to use *tu* with me, or to call me Marston—though I used their first names and the familiar pronoun in talking with them. They felt it disrespectful and said they could not bring themselves to do it. In Puerto Rico on the other hand, at least in intellectual circles, everyone seemed to use both the first name and *tu* from the first introduction—a usage similar to that of American undergraduates.

But the problem of how to talk is relatively simple compared with the problem of how to dress: here too we have the question of what is natural; and even more, the question of what is proper.

X ❧ Covering Up:
What to Wear

One of the most ignominious acts in a man's life is repeated daily when he puts on his trousers. I know of no garment more detrimental to his natural dignity than those limp tubes into which he inserts his legs. Is there anything in the world more limp than an empty pair of trousers? . . . I believe that the decline of civilization set in when [men] began to wear trousers. Now the fall of it seems imminent since women, too, have taken to them.

ROBERT GIBBINGS,
Over the Reefs and Far Away

WHAT SHOULD I wear? This, as every husband knows, is always a problem for our women. But it is a problem for men too; though perhaps not so serious, because the rules are more clear-cut and because there is less variety of choice. The business or professional man automatically puts on a suit when he goes to the office, and his only problems are to decide which suit, shirt and necktie. On Saturday he most likely will wear blue jeans if he plans to cut the lawn—playing at being a laborer and dressing for the part.

Writers, artists—and professors—have greater freedom, and consequently more serious decision-problems each morning. They can wear sports jackets to get that tweedy look—a pipe helps too. If they are daring and reasonably secure, they may even go to work wearing open shirts or, instead of neckties, use those metal ornaments on shoestrings that have lately become a fairly common substitute. These, further, give the poor male a chance to wear a bit of jewelry.

This relative freedom is the cause of my daily dressing problem, mentioned at the beginning of this book. I have been a professor now for some twelve years, and I notice that each year I relax a little more, taking advantage of this aspect of academic freedom—though it may be, of course, that I am simply getting more eccentric as I grow older.

Before coming to the University of Michigan, I had an office for a few years in Rockefeller Center in New York but I lived in Connecticut. During the hot summers I watched the behavior of my fellow-commuters with some amusement: as soon as they got on the train they would take off their coats and ties, only to put them on again at Grand Central Station. I presume that when they got to their offices they would again take them off. But why be properly dressed only between train and office, anonymously, among strangers? I can only think that it was to proclaim professional status, though I doubt whether New York cab drivers would be impressed. I watched this with amusement— but I did the same.

I would probably never have worked up the courage to try rebelling against this routine if my wife had not egged me on. She suggested that I stop talking about how other people behave and start acting more sensibly myself. So one day I went in to the office wearing an open sport shirt and not even carrying a jacket over my arm to show I owned one. Nothing happened. They even let me eat in the lunchroom—restaurants are always a hazard for the unjacketed. Nothing happened with such force that I began to feel extremely uncomfortable. It was almost as though I were having some sort of fit, with everyone carefully not noticing. I didn't have the courage to try again next day—I wore a proper summer suit. I did repeat the experiment a few times later in the summer, always with the same result, but I never did manage to be bold enough to go coatless two days in a row. I suppose if one of my colleagues had caught the infection, I would have gained courage; but everyone else continued to wear proper clothes. Jackets and ties, it seemed, were necessary to support the dignity of an executive position.

A case like this shows clearly enough that physical comfort is a minor consideration in the design of clothing: the only reason I can see for the warm-weather necktie and jacket is status identification. Of course ornament also enters in: the necktie and the clothing materials may well reflect the taste or vanity of the wearer. In this, as in some other respects, we might as well extend the idea of "clothing" to include any attempt at improving on physical appearance: jewelry, cosmetics, tattooing, hair arrangement and the like. Clothing has also become deeply involved with sex, serving sometimes for modest concealment— and sometimes for display or advertisement. I suppose we could bridge this ambivalence by listing "sexual provocation" as one of the basic functions of clothing. And then there is undeniably a protective function: protection against the vicissitudes of climate, against thorns and biting insects, against weapons as in the case of medieval armor and against accidents as in the case of helmets for miners and motorcyclists.

We thus have four main classes of functions for clothing: identification, ornament, provocation and protection —each of them in itself varied. We could undoubtedly extend the list beyond these with a number of more minor types of functions. Transport, for instance: there is no denying the utility of pockets, and all sorts of things can be conveniently attached to a belt. Then too, clothing can be used for camouflage, as in jungle warfare or bird-watching. But this could be considered an aspect of the protective function. Most of the minor purposes of clothing could, I suspect, fall within one or another of my four main headings.

In the case of identification, clothing proclaims not only status, but also sex and tribal or cultural or national affiliation. The identification, of course, is not infallible, since individuals may wear clothing inappropriate to their status, their sex, or their cultural background. I suspect that such misdressing is generally conscious and deliberate, sometimes with intent to deceive and sometimes with another motive. But there is also an accidental form of misdressing, as when one makes the mistake of going to a party overdressed.

In civilizations the identifying aspects of clothing may be prescribed by law, and in all cases they are under strong control through custom, or through taboos that are not easily or often broken. With us, sexual identification is governed by law, at least if the intent is to take on the appearance of the opposite sex. I suppose it would generally be illegal, or at least outrageous, for a man to wear a skirt, but women these days are increasingly taking to trousers. As I was writing this my oldest daughter came into the room, wearing fly-front blue jeans and a man's T-shirt; nowadays, I have learned, fathers are as apt to lose clothes to their daughters as to their sons. In Marian's case there was still no doubt about sexual identification because of her hair, her make-up and her jewelry, quite aside from an obviously feminine figure.

The cult of male clothing among contemporary girls seems to be in large part a matter of convenience. Pockets are handy, and trousers in most situations are more manageable than skirts and certainly more comfortable in cold weather. There may also be an element of rebellion against the traditionally dependent role of women in our society, symbolized by the peculiarities of their dress. Lawrence

Langner, in his book *The Importance of Wearing Clothes,*
maintains that female dress is the consequence of a male
plot to keep females subordinate. "Contrary to established
beliefs," he writes, "the differentiation in clothing between men and women arose from the male's desire to
assert superiority over the female and to hold her to his
service. This he accomplished through the ages by means of
special clothing which hampered or handicapped the female in her movements. Then men prohibited one sex
from wearing the clothing of the other, in order to maintain this differentiation."

I find this difficult to believe. In my experience, men
have little influence on what women wear—women dress
for one another, and no mere male, unless perhaps a dress
designer, can understand all of the subtleties involved.
It is true that women in many cultures besides our own
wear handicapping clothes, but I suspect this has been their
own idea, to show off, irrelevant to the war between men
and women. After all, men wear handicapping clothes too
—witness that necktie—and the beatnik male counterpart
of the trousered girl wouldn't be caught dead wearing a
necktie. Both sexes are rebelling against traditions, with
results that are sometimes confusing. At least I am sometimes confused on the campus these days, since the boys
have taken to wearing long hair, and the girls to trousers
and little make-up. Youth is rebelling, not a particular
sex.

Our young people are thus tending to break the universal rule among all peoples that wear clothing: that the
dress of the two sexes be distinctive. Sex identification
has been a basic function of clothing, which is curious because without any clothing at all the two sexes are easily
enough distinguished in the human species. But just as
sexual difference in clothing is universal, so, it is said, is
transvestism, the reversing of the clothing pattern. In many
cultures this is not only tolerated, but integrated into

cultural and religious practices. The male transvestite, for instance, may go through special ceremonies initiating him into the female role which he wishes to adopt. Accounts of socially accepted male transvestism are particularly common among Indian tribes in both North and South America.

The relationship between transvestism and homosexuality is not as clear as one might at first think. Some clinical psychologists, who ought to know, insist that the two conditions are quite independent. Psychological studies, understandably, have been largely restricted to Western societies, and in our culture it does seem that the desire of a male to wear female clothing, or vice versa, may be quite independent of preference in sexual activity. Transvestites often say they feel more "natural" or more "comfortable" in opposite-sex clothing. This, it develops, may stem from very early childhood experiences: for example, from a mother who, wanting a daughter, dresses her son in girl's clothing at the age of two or three and tells him how "adorable" he looks. One can see that this sort of conditioning might be quite independent of the conditioning arising from early physical experiences with sex, which may be important in determining whether the primary orientation is heterosexual or homosexual.

Yet in our society many male homosexuals like to wear "drag," like to assume complete feminine costume from high-heeled shoes to ear-rings and wig; and many female homosexuals like to wear severely masculine clothes. These make our stereotype of the "queen" or the "bulldyke" and they are at least common enough to have given rise to the stereotype.

Our society is peculiar, as has often been remarked, in that the women dress more gaudily than the men. Males in general throughout the animal kingdom constitute the gaudy sex, with only sporadic exceptions, and this is also true among most peoples. Even with us, males show off whenever they get a chance: witness the dress uniforms of the military, and academic or religious regalia. And male dress in Europe was at least as elaborate as that of the females until the beginning of the nineteenth century. What happened to deprive the poor Western male of his plumage?

The most common explanation is the rise of democracy, the spread of feelings of equality that found its most dramatic expression in the French Revolution. I don't suppose we can blame the Revolution directly for our loss of finery, though the sansculottes were certainly against all outward show of rank and fortune and in favor of plain clothing. Reaction to the violence of the Revolution might have led to an increase in the complexity of clothing, except that in all European countries there was a strong trend toward lessening the outward signs of rank. And the elaborate costumes of earlier years, the wigs and lace and endless curlicues (clear evidence that the wearer did not have to work), were certainly for gentlemen and not for laborers.

The curious thing is why the simplification of clothing was so long confined to the male sex. The elaborately corseted and petticoated women continued to show convincingly that they did not have to work. Only in recent years has the simplification of women's dress gained momentum, along with the increasing pressures for equal rights for women in all respects. And they are still allowed to wear the jewelry, the make-up, and the painted fingernails denied to men. Maybe the male transvestite is sometimes only hankering after the gaudiness that in most societies and in most times has been allowed his sex. The trouble with this theory is that male gaudiness seems to have little appeal for the females in our society—though I sometimes wonder about that too when I see the shirts that my wife buys for me.

But even the simplified and dull male dress of our cul-

ture still serves to identify rank—as the episode with which
I began this chapter shows—and this has been an important function of clothing in most times and places. This is
especially true if one uses clothing in the broadest sense,
including such things as the crown and scepter of a king,
the comb in the hair of a Micronesian chief, or the caste
marks of a Hindu. In general, the more costly and complex the costume, the higher the rank—clothes becoming
another way in which the general human tendency to show
off wealth or prestige can find expression.

Attempts have often been made to control who can wear
what by means of sumptuary laws. These hardly work in
the modern democratic world except for organizations
like the military or the church, and one explanation of
fashion is that it is an attempt to keep class distinctions
in dress. Those in the know—and those that can afford to
—can follow the latest mode, thus maintaining a subtle
distinction between themselves and people with less money
or less knowledge of what is currently appropriate. As
styles drift downward through the social strata, the inno-
vators can always keep ahead with some new twist to show
how sophisticated they are.

Proper clothes, of course, must be worn on solemn occasions and in solemn places—churches and law courts. I
don't know whether the American Medical Association has
a rule that physicians must wear neckties, but I don't recall
ever seeing a physician in his office without jacket and tie.
Medical schools in general require students to wear ties
along with their white jackets as part of their training for
future high status. For that matter, many universities require students to be properly dressed for meals or on other
specified occasions. Then there are the many restaurants,
bars and clubs that require coats and/or ties for admission,
keeping spares to lend to men who come unprepared. The
object is to show that they are high-class joints. A puzzling
case here is that of the exclusive private clubs that require

proper clothes of their members and guests. One would think that the rigorous screening of the membership committees would be assurance enough of high status, without the requirement of outward sign.

The extreme of explicit identification through clothing is reached with uniforms. These are classed by J. C. Flügel, in his book *The Psychology of Clothes,* as a variety of "fixed costume," in contrast with the "modish costume" subject to the vagaries of fashion. Academic and ecclesiastical robes show clearly enough how some types of costume can remain fixed for long periods of time. Military uniforms change, but slowly and for reasons unrelated to fashion—or sense. It was only as late as the Boer War that the British really seemed to understand that bright uniforms make excellent targets, and turned to khaki. Germany, Italy, the United States and other countries then did the same, each country adopting a somewhat different shade. Dress uniforms however remain gaudy enough, and bright spots of color are added by medals, service stripes and the like.

All clothes have some effect on the wearer's psychology: the smug feeling of being perfectly dressed, the open rebellion of beards and sandals, the misery of having inadvertently worn the wrong thing. But I think the psychological effect reaches the extreme with the uniforms of people in governmental service: military, police, customs and the like. Even the meek become fierce when properly uniformed: a phenomenon that might be called the warpaint syndrome. Of course indoctrination goes along with the uniform, and there is always the possibility that authoritarian or sadistic personalities tend to adopt roles in which they can wear uniforms. But even if this is true, there is likely a reinforcing effect. Langner suggests that "A disarmament conference which resulted in a general agreement to prohibit the use of soldiers' uniforms as contrary to international law might possibly bring the world closer to universal peace than any other measure!"

A uniform—that is, one form—serves to subordinate the individual to the group. This is true of the soldier, the sailor or the policeman; but it is also true of the waitress, the nurse, the bellboy (and the prisoner). I have often looked wonderingly at members of service groups, thinking, "These are people, individuals; why can't they express their personalities in their clothing?" But I suppose the management knows what it is doing: it doesn't want personalities waiting on the tables, though the personality often comes through despite the uniformity of the uniforms.

Local, regional and national costumes form another category of "fixed" dress that is relatively free from the changes of fashion, yet allows greater freedom for individual taste than the rigidly prescribed uniform. Regional costume is often not only attractive and colorful, but well adapted to climate and occupation. I think it is one of the unfortunate aspects of the modern world that regional costumes are rapidly tending to disappear, or to be worn only on holidays or to amuse gawking tourists. I blame this on the arrogance of Western civilization, which, for a few hundred years, has been able to push much of the rest of the world around and which has tended to regard any dress other than its own as, at best, quaint. Non-western peoples, impressed with our technical accomplishments, seem also to assume that our clothes, somehow, have something to do with our progress, and they have taken to trousers, jackets and ties as symbols of it.

One trouble is that Western dress, at least for the male, is much less colorful, less ornamental, than the dress of other cultures, and ornament is a basic function of clothing. One theory is that clothing started as ornament, as one aspect of the universal tendency of the human animal to try to improve on his natural body. Along with painting and scarring his skin and trimming or arranging his hair, primitive man surely also took to hanging things around his neck and waist, wrists and ankles. Things hung around the neck or waist could easily, through enlargement, evolve into something we would recognize as dress—the cloak or the loincloth.

For a long time this seemed to me the most likely explanation of clothing, but I have begun to have doubts. Clothing is clearly only one form of the general phenomenon of body modification. Flügel, in his book on clothes, recognizes two main forms of body decoration: corporal, modification of the skin or physique itself; and external, things added on, like clothes or jewelry. His main headings under corporal decoration are cicatrisation ("embellishment by means of scars"), tattooing, painting, mutilation and deformation. Some of these, especially the scarring and the mutilations, are very painful. While it is obvious enough that people nowadays will go to a great deal of trouble and pain to achieve what they think is an improvement in appearance, it is hardly likely that this would be so at the beginning of the process, and some of the mutilations seem to have long histories.

More and more I am coming to believe that the various forms of clothing and body modification started for superstitious reasons, though it bothers me to ascribe so much that is purely human to superstition rather than reason. But the mutilations—circumcision, subincision, clitoridectomy, the knocking out of teeth, the scarring of the face or body—are most frequently associated with the initiation rites of puberty, and along with other ordeals, symbolize the attainment of adult status. The only one of these mutilations that has persisted into civilization is circumcision, which is now quite widely practiced in early infancy for allegedly hygienic reasons. There is little doubt about its ritual origins, and some people maintain that the current vogue in the United States represents medical fashion rather than sound hygiene.

Body painting and tattooing are also often associated with initiation or with other ceremonial occasions, and clothing itself is deeply involved with ceremony. I am thus coming to believe that the origins of clothing and body ornamentation or mutilation, like the origins of dance, music and art, are all tied together and enmeshed with the beginnings of religion. How all this came about, however, is beyond my imagining.

Ornament and sex, of course, are all mixed up, which brings us to what I called the provocative function of clothing: covering up to hide, or draping things on the body to show off. Our attitude toward clothing, as Flügel has pointed out, is truly ambivalent in the psychoanalytic sense of the word. He observes that "we are trying to satisfy two contradictory tendencies by means of our clothes, and we therefore tend to regard clothes from two incompatible points of view—on the one hand, as a means of displaying our attractions, on the other hand, as a means of hiding our shame. Clothes, in fact, as articles devised for the satisfaction of human needs, are essentially in the nature of a compromise; they are an ingenious device for the establishment of some degree of harmony between conflicting interests. In this respect the discovery, or at any rate the use, of clothes seems, in its psychological aspects, to resemble the process whereby a neurotic symptom is developed. Neurotic symptoms, as it is the great merit of psychoanalysis to have shown, are also something of a compromise, due to the interplay of conflicting and largely unconscious impulses."

Clothes, then, represent a neurosis. I like that, and I think it does explain a great deal of our irrationality about clothes. Why is it so terribly embarrassing for a man to find that the fly of his trousers is open, even though his sexual equipment is equally well concealed whether the fly is open or not? Why are swimming trunks all right on the beach, but not in town, even on a hot day? Why can't we run around the house in our underwear when visitors are present? For that matter, why do we even have to have the underwear? But such questions go on endlessly: my next thought is, why does the pubic hair have to be removed from the photograph of a nude woman?

The psychologists are apt to have answers to all such questions, and their answers are apt to involve some aspect of sex. Perhaps they are right, since sex seems to lurk everywhere in our culture; but the relationship sometimes seems far-fetched, at least at first glance. Flügel maintains, for instance, that clothes not only serve to arouse sexual interest, but may also symbolize the sexual organs. He feels that we still have a great deal to learn about this aspect of psychology, but goes on to say, "We know, however, that a great many articles of dress, such as the shoe, the tie, the hat, the collar, and even larger and more voluminous garments, such as the coat, the trousers, and the mantle may be phallic symbols, while the shoe, the girdle, and the garter (as well as most jewels) may be corresponding female symbols."

The idea of the shoe as a phallic symbol struck me as ridiculous, but Flügel makes a plausible case. He points out that at one time during the Middle Ages there was a tendency to fashion the long shoe in the actual shape of a phallus—and that this tendency remains in the unnatural shape of modern shoes. I have often wondered about the shape of our shoes because it is so ill-adapted to the form of the feet, which tend to be broadest at the toes—a fact that the Japanese recognize in shaping their sandals. Maybe Flügel has something.

Lawrence Langner, in his book on clothes, goes even farther than Flügel with sexual associations. He thinks that clothes may have started because the human male, walking upright, needed to find some way of protecting his exposed genitals from the hazards of the environment, and that the apron may well have been the first garment invented by man. Once the genitals were hidden, curiosity started its work: everyone presumably wondering what everyone else's genitals looked like. Langner goes so far as to consider that man's continuous sexuality may be a consequence of this covering up of the sexual organs. He notes, "As the result of inventing and wearing clothes (and undoubtedly an unexpected result), man has been able to impart an important stimulus to the mating instinct which has helped to make this all-the-year-round mating continuously interesting. . . ."

Langner thinks that peoples that habitually go naked are less interested in sex than those that cover up. This, I think, would be difficult to prove. I have the impression, from anthropological reading, that societies vary greatly in their attitudes toward sex and in the amount of time dedicated to sexual activity, unrelated to habits of dress. Our society certainly is much preoccupied with sex and also much addicted to covering up, and the two are clearly related. The same could be said of North African and Near Eastern Muslim cultures—though the clothes and the preoccupations are different. But I think this is explicable in terms of the histories of these particular cultures, rather than as a reflection of some universal law.

Langner cites the high moral tone of nudist colonies in support of his contention, and nudists may maintain that going without clothes cools the libido, among other things. But the high moral tone is also the consequence of deliberate policy. The nudist cult has trouble enough with the law as it is, and any suspicion of immorality would result in the closing of the camps. Individuals wishing to join a nudist group are screened carefully for respectability, and much attention is given to the maintenance of decorum in the camps. Alcoholic drinks, for instance, are usually not allowed. A drunken nudist orgy, then—which might be lots of fun—would have to be arranged privately on some hidden estate, and would never get into the statistics unless by way of a Kinsey interview.

Nudists claim that divorce, sexual misbehavior, sex offenses and juvenile delinquency are less common in their groups than in the general population, and they attribute these virtues to their habit of going without clothes. I am a nudist at heart and I love to take my clothes off whenever the place and the weather permit, but I don't think this contributes to my moral respectability.

The modern nudist movement started in Germany shortly before the First World War and it proliferated greatly there after the war, until Hitler put an end to it. It has revived since the Second World War, but not to the previous extent. German nudism was closely associated with socialism; as L. C. Hirning remarks in his article on "Clothing and Nudism" in the *Encyclopedia of Sexual Behavior,* "An extreme uniformity and simplicity in dress and nonconformity in the philosophy of clothes accompanied nonconformity in social and political thought." This relation between nudism and worker movements has never developed in English-speaking countries. Nudists in England and the United States are generally middle class and conventional enough except for this one quirk.

There has been a gradual liberalization of the laws relative to the practice of nudism in the United States in recent years, paralleling the relaxation of the laws about obscenity. Only three states now have antinudist laws, according to Dr. Hirning. Again the chief antagonist of the nudist movement has been the Post Office, ever zealous about American morals. The postal authorities are particularly horrified by photographs showing male genitals or female pubic hair. The "Post Office" of course really means particular individuals who are able, as Dr. Hirning remarks, to "hide their prejudices, irrationalities, and unconscious motivations behind the anonymity of a government agency." He further notes, "An analysis of the reasons for this outstanding zeal on the part of the postal authorities lies in the realm of clinical investigation beyond the scope of this article."

The nudists—and many nude or scantily clothed primitive peoples—show clearly enough that we can be comfortable in reasonable climates without the protection of clothes. The naked Indians of Tierra del Fuego and the naked blackfellows of Tasmania and southern continental Australia indicate that man can survive in freezing weather without clothes, if he is used to it—though I find it hard to believe that these people are really comfortable, naked in the sleet. But in most environments we have undoubtedly exaggerated the protective function of clothing. Westerners, in fact, would probably be healthier if they wore fewer clothes—one of the nudists' arguments.

There is no denying, however, that clothes do protect the body, even though this function may generally be subordinate to the functions of ornament, provocation and identification. I remember in Micronesia, in my first enthusiasm for the warm South Pacific climate, cutting the legs off all my trousers. I soon regretted this as my legs got scratched in the pandanus thickets, and I was very thankful presently to get a shipment of materials that included some unamputated trousers. Yet the natives seemed to get along all right without covering up their legs; maybe it was just that civilization had made me effete.

Human life would obviously be impossible in the arctic without the fitted Eskimo garment; and loose, draped, Arab-like clothes are protective in the hot, dry tropics. Then we have clothes for protection against our fellow-men—leather and metal armor, and bulletproof vests—and helmets and goggles for protection against accidents.

But, as Flügel has pointed out, beyond this physical protection there is a psychological protection, which in many circumstances may be even more important.

I have already suggested that clothing and ornament may have started for superstitious reasons—what Flügel calls protection against spirits and the "evil eye." We have pretty well got over this, though many of us still cling to small superstitions about ornaments and garments; but we have developed a whole new set of fears and anxieties against which our clothes serve as some protection. Flügel lists the factors that enter into our present associations as follows:

1. Color. We equate black with seriousness; white with innocence and moral purity; while the brighter spectral colors signify a freer play of the emotions.

2. Amplitude. Insofar as we feel that the body is evil, we escape its dangers by covering up as much as possible.

3. Thickness. Flügel thinks that the real protective value of thick clothes against certain physical dangers may be unconsciously extended to protection against moral dangers.

4. Stiffness. We associate physical stiffness in garments (the starched shirt of evening dress) with uprightness and firmness; loose, slack and sloppy clothes become associated with corresponding ways of life.

5. Tightness. Here there is the actual physical support of tight garments; but as Flügel observes, this is easily transferred to the moral sphere, the tightness symbolizing a firm control over ourselves ("keeping a tight rein on our passions").

Flügel's associations between clothing and attitudes seem to me reasonable enough, except for the last. I have the impression from watching our youth that "tightness" has lost any association with firm moral control, at least in recent years. The girls with tight sweaters are showing off—even though they have tight (or padded?) brassieres underneath. I'm not sure what the boys are doing with their very tight trousers (I sometimes wonder how they manage to get into them), but they hardly seem to symbolize moral control. And then there are the modern bathing suits, skimpy, but also tight—and these too hardly serve for either physical or moral support.

But there we are, all bundled up in our clothes, more or less protected from the world around us. This, as Langner points out, helps us to think we are god-like, different from the naked animal world we would like to transcend. But the method of achieving this spiritual protection—the kind of clothes that we put on—depends on the group of people with which we identify. We are thus back at the beginning, with clothing as identification, with the problem of sorting out the varied cultures and subcultures that have developed within our species.

XI ❧ *Subcultures and Contracultures*

> The idea that a group can suddenly be emancipated from its past habits is no more sensible than the idea that a man who flaps his arms rapidly enough can fly.
>
> STUART CHASE,
> *The Proper Study of Mankind*

"*CULTURE*" in the anthropological sense is not an easy word to define, though anthropologists have invested a great deal of energy in the attempt. Alfred L. Kroeber and Clyde Kluckhohn produced a whole book based on an analysis of some hundreds of definitions (*Culture: A Critical Review of Concepts and Definitions*). Yet it is easy enough to get the idea of what is meant by the word: a particular way of life characterizing a group of people. The "society" is the people; the "culture," their way of life. Often there is not much of a problem in identifying cultures, since we tend to be specific. We do not refer to American Indian culture, but to that of the Navajo, the Hopi, or some such particular tribe. This is generally true for tribal groups; difficulties enter with the complexities of civilization.

Is Western civilization a single culture, or a series of differing cultures? It probably matters little which alternative is taken, but I prefer to think of it as a single, though endlessly diverse, cultural entity. In doing this I am using "culture" as roughly equivalent to the idea of "civilization" as developed by Arnold Toynbee in *A Study of History*. Toynbee's civilization is an "intelligible field of study": a unit that can be described and understood with a minimum of reference outside. Great Britain, for instance, is not such an entity, because its history cannot be told without frequent reference to events across the Channel. The "intelligible field of study" is Western Europe as a whole. On the other hand, Chinese history up until modern times can be discussed without any mention of events in Europe: it represented a separate and distinct civilization.

Toynbee's definition applies as well to the cultural concept in general as it does to the special case of civilizations. Protestants, Catholics, British, European Jews, university professors and students—the endlessly diversifying traditions and attitudes that have developed within the West —cannot be understood without constant reference to one another. But in studying these we need pay little attention to the ideas of Brahmins, mandarins or coolies.

Western civilization has gained cultural unity from its Graeco-Roman origins, from the common heritage of Christian tradition, from the frequent interaction of its members and from the network of economic ties and ideas resulting from the Industrial Revolution and the development of science. Yet this culture—this civilization—is fragmented by languages, nationalisms, religions, occupations and the like. Within any national society such as the United States or Great Britain there is a bewildering constellation of subgroupings, of subcultures, often only vaguely distinguishable. But in many important respects these subcultures govern the behavior, the ideas, the attitudes of individuals.

There are a number of recognizable subcultures that have in common a rebellion against some aspect of the system of beliefs held by the majority of members of a society. Milton Yinger, in an article published in the

American Sociological Review of October 1960, has proposed calling such groups "contracultures." This seems like a useful idea, though it turns out in practice not always to be easy to apply. As Yinger observes, "The values of most subcultures probably conflict in some measure with the larger culture. In a contraculture, however, the conflict element is central; many of the values, indeed, are specifically contradictions of the values of the dominant culture."

Yinger develops his idea of contraculture with the case of gangs of delinquent youth. Adolescents in general can be considered a subculture within our society: anyone with teen-age children knows the problem of keeping up with their jargon, with their ideas about clothes and about how to spend their leisure time. Memories of one's own adolescence don't help a bit—electric trains have given way to racing slot cars; wide flannels to tight Levis; and vocabulary has changed completely. Youth is probably always rebellious to some extent—and if one looks at adult society with clear eyes, this is understandable enough. There is probably also always some tendency to form clubs, gangs, mutually exclusive ingroups. But usually the behavior is not intentionally destructive or bitterly defiant; in Yinger's terms, the conflict element is not central.

The case is different with the gangs of our city streets that have received so much attention from newspapers, politicians and social scientists. These are clearly contracultural: continually in conflict with the large society in which they find themselves. I tend to agree with Paul Goodman, who, in *Growing Up Absurd*, blames our troubles largely on the way we have allowed our cities to develop. The members of the gangs come from low-income groups (though poverty doesn't necessarily cause delinquency, it certainly contributes), from unstable or broken homes, and they simply have nothing to do and no place to go and no aspirations in our managerial society. The streets where the kids used to play are now full of auto-mobiles, and the jobs they used to get either have been re-placed by machines or are now managed by phony white-collar boys from the suburbs who really don't know any-thing either.

But I am not going to contribute to the literature on delinquency. All I know is what I read in the papers or in novels or in sociology books. I don't know whether delin-quent gangs are increasing in numbers and in threat, or whether they are simply more visible than before. Some-times they seem to me a special case of a class of contra-cultures that has long been with us—the outlaw societies. You can't blame Robin Hood or the Barbary pirates on slums or slum clearance—though there is always some reason for alienation from the large society.

It looks as if every civilization has had contracultural outlaw groups: organized rebellion by minorities against the rules of the society. Such groups tend to proliferate when the government is weak or dissolute, and in the con-fused aftermath of wars. Thus the most famous of the out-law groups of the modern West, the Camorra of Naples and the Mafia of Sicily, had their origins in the disorder following the Napoleonic invasion of Italy early in the nineteenth century. In the case of the Mafia, "Lawless conditions led the owners of large estates to place their lands in the charge of energetic ruffians who exercised al-most despotic powers over a terrorized peasantry" (quot-ing the *Encyclopaedia Britannica*). The "ruffians" pres-ently turned on the landlords as well as the peasants, and also began to terrorize the towns. Bands often feuded among themselves, but efforts of the Italian government at suppression were ineffective until after the establish-ment of the Fascist regime.

The Mafia is said to be still with us in the United States. Authors differ in estimating its importance: it is difficult to be authoritative about secret criminal organizations. Also, a group like the Mafia tends to try to take credit for any act of violence as a way of inflating its power. But whatever the role of the Mafia in this country, there is no doubt that we have, and have had, plenty of contracultural criminal groups.

From the beginning of North American settlement, individuals and groups disgruntled with constituted authority, or running afoul of it, could escape to the open western regions, sometimes joining with the Indians, sometimes preying upon them. After the Revolution, the War of 1812 and the Mexican War, the outlaw bands grew with the addition of ex-soldiers who had failed to adjust to civilian life. But it was not until their numbers were swelled with Civil War veterans that these bands became a real threat to the development of the region, giving rise to the Wild West of legend and history.

The supposedly free life of the outlaw has always had an appeal to those constrained by the dull realities of organized society—this might be called the Robin Hood complex—and a number of the desperadoes of our West received a certain amount of hero worship in the East. They still have this glamour, for that matter, in movies, television and comic books.

The West was gradually cleaned up as states were organized and law-enforcement agencies established. Then we had our next great spree of outlawry with the days of prohibition. Bootlegging became such a vast enterprise that it led to the formation of national criminal syndicates, which are said to be still with us. One wonders whether Americans have an unusual tolerance for lawlessness, or whether we are unusually addicted to passing laws which have no support from large parts of the population. I suspect the latter: witness the difference between law and practice in relation to such things as gambling, drugs and prostitution.

Can one say that prostitutes constitute a contraculture? Certainly they do not conform to the expressed values of our society, but their rebellion is individual, and their interaction is not so much with one another as with their clients. The prostitute-client relationship is too furtive and shifting to have any of the characteristics of a social group. Besides, the clients are apt to be perfectly respectable people, apparently subscribing to all of the accepted values of the culture, except that their sexual impulses sometimes get the upper hand.

I am thinking of the situation in the United States today. In London, judging from the description given by Wayland Young in his book *Eros Denied*, there is more social interaction among prostitutes, and they and their ponces might well be considered to form a definable contraculture: contra because their way of life is openly condemned by the articulate majority and is, in fact, illegal. In countries where their profession is perfectly legal, prostitutes often are sociable enough with one another— but if their activity is accepted by the society, they could hardly be said to be in conflict. Prostitution as a way of life may not be highly esteemed by the governing classes, but it is not apt to be condemned by "common people" in societies where the Puritan tradition is not dominant.

I have never been able to understand the attitude of our society toward prostitution. For the most part it may be a pretty dismal way of life—but we have many other dismal occupations. I can't see any basic difference between selling your body for sex and selling it for baseball or football; or for that matter, selling the ability to write or draw. With sex, the line between giving a dinner or a trinket and giving cash seems particularly thin. There is, of course, a value system that would condemn any action carried out for money rather than for love; but this value system, however estimable, gets at most lip service from our society.

A recent book by Harry Benjamin and R. E. L. Masters, *Prostitution and Morality*, points out that many of our attitudes toward prostitution are based on myths: the moralists have been hoodwinking us again, and creating vice and misery by attempting to suppress them. The whole "white slave" thesis has little basis in fact in modern times, though where slavery has been institutionalized some slaves were forced into prostitution, just as others were forced to be carpenters or farm hands. I think the whole thing is best summed up in a quotation given by Benjamin and Masters from H. L. Mencken's *In Defense of Women*: "The truth is that prostitution is one of the most attractive of the occupations practically open to the sort of women who engage in it, and that the prostitute commonly likes her work, and would not exchange places with a shop-girl or a waitress for anything in the world."

I suspect that prostitutes, where their profession is illegal, suffer a great deal from police harassment and from the need to conceal their activities. This may often lead to the association of prostitution with other illegal activities. Customers too must often be unpleasant characters —but this is a hazard with any occupation.

Let's get back to the comparison between food and sex. We could hardly expect good meals and sanitary preparation if restaurants were illegal. I sometimes try to imagine the furtive conversations with a taxi driver in a strange city about where to find a good beefsteak, and all of the rackets and payoffs that would be involved. People have been selling both food and sex for a long time now; but at least we can still be reasonably sure that the cook is not a typhoid carrier, and that the dishes have been washed, whereas venereal disease has lately been increasing alarmingly, as have illegitimate pregnancies.

The case of prostitutes brings to mind that of homosexuals. There is, in our major cities, a "gay world" that has been described in considerable detail in a number of recent books, both fiction and nonfiction. The homosexuals have a special jargon which is rather uniform and widely known over the country—though in view of those recent books, it is no longer a very private language. There are special bars which they frequent, and in some cases, groups manage a quite complex social life, with cocktail parties, dinners and the like. This form of sex is definitely in conflict with the overtly expressed values of our society and is, in fact, illegal almost everywhere. Police can easily show how efficient they are by raiding gay bars to round up sexual perverts, making an impressive record with no trouble at all—though what they protect society from by this process is not clear.

Does this make a contraculture? This was my first impression; but the more I have thought about it, read about it and talked about it, the less convinced I am. A tendency toward homosexual behavior seems to be a personality trait, likely to characterize individuals in many different walks of life. The "gay society" of a large city may be cohesive enough and apart enough to be considered a special subculture, but the members of the group generally conform to the values of the society except in the one matter of sexual behavior. I have been taken to cocktail parties in New York and in San Francisco where everyone present was said to be gay: but it would be difficult to imagine a more respectable group of people, not only in appearance, but (disappointingly) also in behavior. I suspect that such people, overly conscious of their one deviation from the accepted norm, tend to compensate by a more rigid conformity in other respects. I am thinking now of people who are lawyers, accountants, executives—people with primary allegiance to some business or professional group. Artists, writers, actors and the like apparently can afford to be more nonconforming both in dress and be-havior; but this is true whatever the nature of their sexual inclinations.

The homosexual residents of Park Avenue are people who, in the terms of our society, would be classed as suc-cessful—which in itself would keep them from being grouped as a contraculture, despite (in Yinger's terms) the central nature of their conflict with expressed social values. There are, of course, many other kinds of homo-sexual groups: the hustlers, for instance, but they can no more be called a cohesive group than can their female prostitute counterparts; and the screaming faggots who flaunt their femininity on the street or in bars and who indeed might be considered to form a contraculture ex-cept that their rebellion is not so much against society as against their masculine role in it. Then there are the thwarted, the people one of my friends calls "ribbon-clerk queens," who use their sexuality as an excuse for relative failure but still cling pathetically to the trappings of re-spectability. I suppose they could not be said to form a contraculture as long as they keep trying. The truly de-feated, whether by sex or by some other aspect of their personality or of society, make up the membrship of skid row; they are the bums. Do they form a contraculture?

A book by Donald Bogue, *Skid Row*, summarizes a thor-ough sociological study of Chicago's bums. The picture that emerges from this study is hardly that of a definite contraculture; it is rather that of an aggregation of dere-licts, of individuals who for varied reasons have not been able to cope with ordinary society. They are all poor, they are mostly older men with no family life, and they have acute personal problems. But they are not necessarily re-bellious against the society into which they could not fit. The Chicago workers tried specifically to get a measure-ment of conformity. They found that "only 3 per cent of all homeless men could be classified as definite nonconformists by the coders, while there was evidence that 47 per cent were conformists. An additional 43 per cent were categorized as not strongly influenced by custom, but not rebellious."

One tends to think of skid row as inhabited by drunks; but the Chicago study found 14.8 per cent of the men to be teetotalers, and only 12.6 per cent to be "alcoholic derelicts"—though as Bogue points out, "it is abundantly clear that 30–35 per cent of the men on Skid Row definitely fall in the 'problem drinker' category." Alcoholism, then, however important it may be, is not the explanation for skid row; neither is criminal behavior. Jackrollers and pickpockets are there, preying on the drunks and on visitors; and outside criminals use it as a temporary hiding place. But it is peripheral to the general criminal contraculture—life there would be too uncomfortable for a thief with any ability at all. Skid row thus appears to be a rather clearly defined subculture within our civilization, characterized by extreme poverty and by the inability of its members to adjust to social norms—but the inability to adjust has not led to the conscious rebellion and defiance of a contraculture.

The idea of a rebellious contraculture makes one think of the case of Negroes in our society. If any group has cause for rebellion, it is they. But Negroes cannot be lumped into any single cultural category: the only defining characteristic, as we use the term in the United States, is evidence of some share of colored ancestry, usually showing in terms of skin color, hair form, or perhaps facial features. Such traits hardly define a way of life; but they can be and are used as caste marks, serving as identification to the dominant group in enforcing limitations on activity. Any sharing of a way of life by the colored population exclusively is thus imposed from the outside.

The segregation of Negroes as second-class citizens results incidentally in a certain permissiveness: they are not expected to conform to the expressed standards of the dominant society, and often they do not. The result is a certain freedom to be happy-go-lucky, or even shiftless. I have come to feel at home in a few colored bars (in the summer I get dark enough to pass) and the people there seem much freer, more open, and livelier and noisier than their counterparts in paleface bars ("white" is hardly the appropriate adjective). Enviously, I have sometimes asked my colored friends about the value of this freedom from the puritanical tradition. They have always said that any gain was not worth the cost, and I am sure they are right.

The happy-go-lucky stereotype imposes an added burden on colored families striving for respectability. They have to be, or think they have to be, terribly proper. This division in itself makes it impossible for anything that could be called a "colored subculture" to form: the social distinctions within the colored population are as great as those within any part of our society. The difference between a professional man and a day laborer does not depend on skin color—although in our culture skin color becomes a sensitive, added hazard in life.

Over the years I have become more and more indignant about the "race" question in the United States, and I can document some of the steps in this increasing indignation. I was brought up in southern Florida, but somehow missed worrying about race—or about any kind of social problem for that matter. Then I lived for three years in the Caribbean after college, and became very concerned about misunderstandings between the United States and Latin America—a subject that still bothers me greatly—but one is hardly aware of race as a problem in Spanish-speaking countries. My conscious indignation about our attitude toward skin color started one afternoon in Cairo. We were living in the suburb of Ma'adi and one of our neighbors was a Coptic lady, one of the large Egyptian landowners—about the only landowner I met who was deeply and intelligently concerned about Egyptian social conditions. She had traveled widely, but never mentioned the United States, and that afternoon I asked her if she had ever been there. She said no, because she understood it could be difficult—and I suddenly realized for the first time that her skin was very dark. This was in the prewar days when even swank New York hotels and restaurants were unpredictable on race attitudes.

Another step occurred one day in the course of a conversation with a psychiatrist. He said he had learned not to give a Negro deep therapy because, while it might uncover the cause of the immediate problem, it was also likely to bring out a collection of childhood hurts that had been covered up and consciously forgotten. Whenever I see a colored child in this country I think of that remark, and wonder what hurts he has had or will have. This is simply another aspect of the human tendency to be mean, on which Americans have no monopoly. But I do wish I had a clearer idea of how attitudes could rapidly be changed.

One Negro group, the Black Muslims, does have a definite program. These people have decided that the so-called whites are completely hopeless, and that the only solution is segregation of Negroes into separate states. Because of their attitude toward the dominant European culture of our society, the Black Muslims might well be classed as a contraculture. They differ strikingly from other contracultures, however, in having no criminal aspect, except for some of the fringe elements. They are dedicated to discipline, sobriety, industry and all of the other standard virtues of our culture. They just don't like whites and think there is no possibility of compromising with them. Maybe they are right. I have often thought that if I were obviously Negro, I would move to some other country, preferably somewhere in Latin America. Yet there is the experience of James Baldwin, described in *Notes of a Native Son*: Baldwin discovered, while living in Europe, that he was an American, even though a Negro. Maybe there is no geographical escape.

Then there are the Jews—or perhaps better, people with Jewish background, since the identification does not necessarily depend on present religion. Certainly there are recognizable Jewish subcultures, but they have no contracultural aspects despite the long history of ghettos and persecution. There are still anti-Semitic prejudices in the dominant white Protestant culture of the United States, but they seem feeble compared with the anti-Negro prejudice. My impression is that much of the cohesiveness of Jewish subcultures in this country is due to shared heritages: that the relationships arise spontaneously within the groups instead of being forced on them from the outside.

Jewish subcultures have in common a religious heritage, Negro subcultures a racial element, the various contracultures some form of conflict with the large society—all of these things influencing in some way the behavior of the individuals belonging to the groups. The subtle nature of this influence has been nicely shown by the studies on American sex habits made by the late Alfred Kinsey and his colleagues. As they point out in the volume on *Sexual Behavior in the Human Male*, "There is no American pattern of sexual behavior, but scores of patterns, each of which is confined to a particular segment of our society. Within each segment there are attitudes on sex and patterns of overt activity which are followed by a high proportion of the individuals in that group; and an understanding of the sexual mores of the American people as a whole is possible only through an understanding of the sexual patterns of all the constituent groups."

The same kind of remarks could equally well be made about food habits, drinking habits, speech, clothing—all aspects of behavior. Kinsey, for convenience, tabulated his statistics in terms of educational level, occupational class, and occupational class of parents, relying mostly on years of education as an index of social position because this information could most easily be determined. Occupational class would probably be more significant in governing behavior, but the boundaries between classes are not always clear.

Kinsey followed the custom of many modern sociologists in recognizing nine occupational classes: underworld, day labor, semi-skilled labor, skilled labor, lower white-collar group, upper white-collar group, professional group, business executive group and extremely wealthy group. An occupational classification of this sort does not, in general, separate distinctive subcultures because of varying national, religious and racial backgrounds. Geography also enters in: a white-collar worker in New England does not necessarily have the same attitudes and behavior as his counterpart in Georgia or California, though the great mobility of contemporary Americans is tending to lessen the impact of geographical differences.

Using occupational groupings like those of Kinsey is really an attempt to distinguish among social classes. These distinctions are real enough in the United States, despite our pretensions, though the differences are not as clear as in some countries, and perhaps not as important as social scientists like to think. But trying to figure out the class structure of society can be a complicated and amusing game—and it does illuminate human relationships.

We have, traditionally, the separation into lower, middle and upper classes—with the middle class forming the backbone of democracy and maintaining the social proprieties. Everyone I have ever heard discuss the subject has considered himself to be middle class—perhaps because neither the uppers nor the lowers worry about such matters. Lloyd Warner, in his now-classic study of the social structure of "Yankee City," divided each of these traditional classes into two, recognizing "lower-lower, upper-lower, lower-middle" and so on. Proper assignment of individuals in such a class structure, however, requires a great deal of sleuthing, and would be impossible in the time available for individual interviews in such studies as those made by the Kinsey group.

Lloyd Warner, as is well known, made his study in Newburyport, Massachusetts—the hometown of the late John P. Marquand. Marquand, in his novel *Point of No Return,* has given the point of view of the guinea pig in such a sociological study, describing how the social scientists looked to one of the townspeople under observation. I think the novel should be read along with *The Social Life of a Modern Community,* by Lloyd Warner and Paul S. Lunt, to get a balanced view of the New England aspect of the human animal in the 1930s. I like, for instance, Marquand's parody of sociological prose: "Typical of a lower-upper family are the Henry Smiths—father, mother, son and daughter. Like other lower-upper families, they dwell on a side street ('side streeters') , yet are received on Mason Street. Mr. Smith, with investment interests in Boston, whose father owned stock in the Pierce Mill, is a member of the Sibley Club, also the Country Club, but is not a member of the Fortnightly Reading Club, belonging only to its lower counterpart, the Thursday Club. Though a member, he has never been an officer of the Historical Society or a Library trustee. His wife, Mrs. Smith, was Miss Jones, a physician's daughter (middle-upper). She runs their home in the lower-upper manner, with the aid of one maid (middle-lower) coming in from outside. The son Tom, a likeable young graduate of Dartmouth, works ambitiously in the office of the Pax Company and is thinking of leaving for a job in Boston. He and his sister Hannah are received by the upper-upper but are not members of the committee for the Winter Assembly . . ."

If any of these social classes corresponds with a recognizable subculture, it is the upper-uppers, and their subculture may well be what some social scientists have come to call the American Establishment—the people of inherited wealth and status who allegedly run the country. I suppose the same people, at the turn of the century, would have made up Society. These upper-uppers, however, are about as difficult to study as their opposites, the members of the criminal underworld. For one thing, they are relatively scarce, which makes the accumulation of statistics difficult; and for another, they are not easily available for long interviews nor easily persuaded to fill out questionnaires. To gain some understanding of them we have to depend mostly on the perceptions of novelists who like to write about the well-born, or on the dicta of such people as Cleveland Amory or Lucius Beebe. One sociologist, however, E. Digby Baltzell, has written a thought-provoking book on *The Protestant Establishment* in which he analyzes the behavior and attitudes of the white Anglo-Saxon Protestant aristocracy of the United States— the "WASPs."

Baltzell believes that there is an Establishment and that it has considerable power—not in a direct sense, because it can hardly determine who is elected to the Congress or to the Presidency, though it can influence events indirectly through financial support. But acceptance by the wealthy and the well-born can be very flattering— and money can mean power. The Establishment, if there be any such thing, certainly is not organized; its coherence depends on the common background of its members— in boarding school, in college (Harvard, Princeton and Yale), and in clubs.

The metropolitan clubs are curious institutions, imitations of the London strongholds of the British aristocracy. They shun any sort of publicity and tend, on the outside at least, to be unostentatious, blending into the neighborhood. The admissions committees, however, are very conscientious, and may ponder a long time before admitting a new member—and the committees are strongholds of racial, ethnic and religious prejudice, which is only slowly breaking down. Others have noted that the clubs have declined greatly in importance in recent years, and I am not at all sure what function they now serve, except for the vague snobbery of belonging. I have noticed lately that when a friend asks you to have lunch with him at his club, it is generally on the grounds of the food there —and certainly the food in the "best" clubs is apt to be very good. But this hardly seems an adequate excuse for such elaborate institutions.

I am not sure about the existence of an American Establishment or about the extent of its power: I have heard the matter argued heatedly both ways. But I do think there is a recognizable upper-upper subculture—and a very odd world it is—including executives, playboys, socialites, and the celebrities that they accumulate. When sitting in the bar of an "exclusive" club and looking at the local fauna, I get the same feeling of strangeness that I sometimes have, at the opposite extreme, in a waterfront bar. I think, in a way, I can understand and sympathize with the people about me—that I have the potential for being either a bum or a pooh-bah. I suppose all of us have. Yet I cannot now accept the values of either subculture. I have rather reluctantly come to realize that my world is that of the so-called intellectuals: that my subculture is Academia.

When we talk about Academia we generally mean the teachers, the professors. The university community includes not only professors, but also students and administrators. All are committed to the education process, but this does not mean that they form a homogeneous society. In fact, the three groups often are at odds with one another. Students in our system get grades, and these grades may be very important for their future, especially for putting off the draft or for admission to medical school, law school or other advanced training. The students are thus understandably anxious to get good grades; but the professor, equally understandably, cannot give everyone "A." If he did, the grades, as an assessment of accomplishment and ability, would lose all meaning. So student and teacher get jockeyed into positions of mutual suspicion and antagonism. I have heard professors remark during vacation periods on how pleasant a place the university was without any students around—and it is indeed more quiet and peaceful.

The misunderstandings between administration and faculty are more difficult to comprehend, but they exist often enough. As a professor, I have never been able to see why an American university needs quite so many administrative officers: large buildings filled with people busily writing memoranda to one another or to the faculty and filing them away or mailing them out. My own university has seven vice-presidents, each, I presume, with a complex of assistants, aides and secretaries. Goodness knows how many deans, associate deans and assistant deans there are, not to mention chairmen of departments with their administrative assistants, and directors of this or that Institute or Center for something-or-other. And they all feel overworked and understaffed. Parkinson's law is clearly operating. The marvel is that the university, despite all of this, somehow manages to keep going.

I sometimes think that the confusion and misunderstandings within the university system are in part the consequence of the existence of dual objectives: education and research. It is commonly said that the good teacher must also be a good researcher; and it would certainly seem that the man who is doing things would be better able to transmit enthusiasm and the excitement of discovery to his students.

Yet there is a conflict. Teaching in large part consists in transmitting the accumulated knowledge of the culture: passing on the tradition. Discovery in part consists of ignoring the tradition, breaking out in new and unthought-of directions. "Academic" has acquired the connotations of conventional, even of trivial; and not without reason. I have often wondered what would have happened if, in the past, literature, painting, music had been in the hands of the professors. Now the universities have become major patrons of the arts; the most easily available subsidy for the artist is a professorship. Science these days is almost entirely in the hands of the universities; but think of the long fight during the nineteenth century to get the universities (outside of Germany) even to admit that the sciences existed: education involved the study of the classics and of classical languages, not the messy world in which people lived.

I don't intend to write a long digression on the nature of the university; but some comment is needed to gain an understanding of the academic subculture. The universities of the Western world, through much of their history, have served as brakes on wild impulses of change: the professor has been dubious about newfangled ideas, remote from the marketplace and the forum. Hence the idea of the ivory tower. But now the professor is supposed to be in the midst of things, advising governments and corporations, designing spacecraft, studying automobile safety devices, composing electronic music. We are trying to convert the brakes into a system for acceleration; and it is not surprising that there are difficulties.

One result is a great diversification within the academic subculture. There are professors of business, of journalism, of physical education, of pharmacy, of social work, as well as professors of physics, chemistry and biology; and there are still professors of history, philosophy, theology and classical literature. The ideal of the scholar remains strong—though sometimes difficult to apply in home economics, poultry husbandry or nursing.

Academia, like any other subculture, includes a great variety of people. There are pressures for conformity, there are the ideals of scholarship and the dedication of teaching; to some extent these mold all individuals within the group. But each professor is also an individual personality, as every student knows. Some appear to be crackpots, others are rather obviously phony, and still others are as square as any junior executive.

XII ❧ Crackpots, Phonies and Squares

> "I is always wondered how square can a round world be."
>
> Howland Owl in WALT KELLY,
> G. O. Fizzickle Pogo

PERSONALITY—the word comes, ultimately, from the classical Latin *persona*, the mask worn by an actor in a drama to indicate his character. And each of us, in truth, wears a mask before the world: that of a good fellow, or perhaps of a mean bastard, or a silly flirt, or a rough bully, or a tender lover. The possible masks are endless and sometimes we have several for use, appropriate to the occasion. All of us, I suppose, sometimes wonder about ourselves, wonder about the reality beneath this surface: and I suppose it is when the surface gets into serious conflict with underlying and suppressed tendencies that we go to see a psychiatrist to try to get ourselves back into adjustment again.

Personality studies have been a popular subject for social science research for many years now, and numerous schemes have been developed by which people can be described and classified. Some of the personality vocabulary has passed over into the common language. We all know what is meant, for instance, if someone remarks that "John is an extrovert" or notes that Harry shows "anal-compulsive behavior," even though we may not have any very profound knowledge of the theories of either Jung or Freud. But no single scheme has won general acceptance, and it seems to me at least that we are far from an understanding of how these personality differences come about.

The controversy over "nature versus nurture" is still not really resolved: it is difficult to be sure to what extent particular personality traits are the consequence of genetic inheritance, and to what extent the consequence of the environmental conditions under which the individual grew up. Many biologists tend to hold some form of genetic determinism—to believe that the individual is the product of his genes and that society can only be improved by some form of differential breeding. This is the eugenics argument. Social workers, on the other hand, tend to be environmentalists, believing especially that antisocial personality traits are the consequence of bad living conditions, and that society can be improved through social action. The truth, as usual, probably lies somewhere between these extremes: each individual is the result of a certain genetic potential finding expression in a particular environmental context—which leaves plenty of room for environmental improvement. I can't get worried about the eugenic argument, because the human gene pool is so diverse that we cannot predict what combinations will occur, let alone which will turn out to be valuable.

For a long time I was pretty much of an environmentalist, believing that personality traits could most easily be explained by the accidents of childhood, by experiences in the family, the school and the neighborhood. My belief was shaken in the course of watching my own children grow up: each is a different personality, and the differences have been apparent since babyhood. Each, of course, has also had a different environment, in the sense that one is the eldest, one the youngest, and so on. Each also has had different experiences: we were most strict in following routines with our first-born, and most relaxed with the youngest, which must often be the case. But I think I can see hereditary components in their personalities, just as I can see them in eye color, complexion or body build.

One trouble is that I cannot put my finger on the personality components, on the elements of character that might be determined by the genes. I can compare the children's photographs with those of ancestors, but I can't photograph their personalities. And despite all of the work of the psychologists, I remain dubious about our efforts to isolate and measure personality traits. Sometimes I think that in these studies we are still in the earth, air, fire and water stage of analysis. The basic elements that are inherited or modified by the environment may be as unobvious as oxygen, hydrogen, nitrogen and the other chemical elements. We rarely see these chemicals in their pure form, and it may well be that we equally rarely come across the elementary personality traits. Genius may be as complex an arrangement of distinct components as is, say, a protein molecule of chemical elements.

If we are still ignorant of the basic components of personality or temperament, it is not from lack of trying to find them. Many efforts, for instance, have been made to relate personality and physique, as in our cultural stereotype of the jolly fat person, or the fiery temper of a redhead. This kind of association goes back to Hippocrates with his *habitus apoplecticus* (thick, strong, muscular) and *habitus phthisicus* (delicate, linear, weak). Galen was building on the ideas of Hippocrates when he developed the theory of the four humors, which dominated Western medicine for such a long time. The words are still with us even though the theory has been abandoned. There is the sanguine type, due to an excess of blood (loves mirth and music, wine and women); the phlegmatic type, due to excess of phlegm (slothful); the choleric type, due to an excess of yellow bile (violent and fierce) ; and the melancholic type, with an excess of black bile (heavy and depressed, with little daring) . The healthy body and the healthy personality were considered to result from a proper balance among these four humors.

It is interesting that Linnaeus, in the middle of the eighteenth century, when he set out to classify all of the animals and plants of the world, resorted to these humors in characterizing the races of mankind. He described American Indians as choleric (red, irascible, upright) ; Europeans as sanguine (white, hopeful, brawny) ; Asiatics as melancholy (yellow, sad, unbending) ; and Africans as phlegmatic (black, calm, lazy) .

Efforts to relate physique and temperament have continued to this day. Rostan in 1828 proposed three basic types: digestive, muscular and respiratory-cerebral. Later, Kretschmer proposed the terms pyknic, athletic and asthenic for types essentially like those Rostan described. In our own day William Sheldon has been the chief exponent of the physique-temperament relationship. He too has invented a new set of terms recognizing three basic components in the human physique: endomorphy, mesomorphy and ectomorphy, corresponding essentially with the fat, muscular and skinny types. He rates individuals on a seven-point scale for each component, and calls the composite the "somatotype." An individual rated as 4–6–1, for instance, would show four degrees of endomorphy, six of mesomorphy and one of ectomorphy (much brawn and little brains) . Sheldon finds three corresponding temperament components, which he calls viscerotonia (digestive viscera preponderant) , somatotonia (muscles preponderant) and cerebrotonia (central nervous system preponderant) .

Sheldon has accumulated a large amount of data, collecting standardized photographs of thousands of individuals, along with personality information; and he has written several thought-provoking books. Social scientists are all aware of his work, and words like ectomorphic and cerebrotonic are commonly bandied about in academic circles—though for the most part this represents a ponderous sort of academic humor. Some students of personality regard Sheldon as completely crackpot, and he in turn tends to be scornful of the theories of clinical psychologists; other students think that he has established a valid and useful theory of personality. The majority, I suspect, feel that "he has something" but are not quite sure what it is that he has. That is my reaction, at least: the system somehow seems too complex to be practical, and at the same time too simple to be real—simple in the sense of depending on the relative development of only three basic components.

It is always interesting to play the game of trying to fit oneself into personality schemes; in Sheldon's case, I find that I agree fairly well with the list of characteristics for the cerebrotonic type. But the fit is not perfect. Snoring, for instance: Sheldon says that if a cerebrotonic "snores at all, which is rare, it will only be in the morning, and then very lightly." Yet my snoring is notorious, and my wife has tried all sorts of cures unavailingly. Sheldon also says that the cerebrotonic finds the effect of alcohol "essentially unpleasant," and this certainly doesn't apply to me. But then each of us represents a mixture of traits, by any scheme of classification.

Indeed most people try to fit themselves into any system of personality analysis that they happen to be reading—we are all always looking for new insights into ourselves. This curiosity probably accounts for the great popularity of psychology courses among undergraduates. It also accounts for the prevalence and persistence of a considerable variety of pseudosciences concerned with the diagnosis of personality. We have phrenology, palmistry, graphology, astrology and the like, as well as plain fortune-telling. I even recently came across a "science of

gynecomammalogy" which relates female breast types to
personality and character.

Phrenology, the science of determining character by
the shape of the skull—by feeling the bumps on the head
—reached a tremendous development in the middle of
the nineteenth century, with millions of devotees. There
were numerous phrenological societies, a number of more
or less learned phrenological journals, and many books.
The idea was that the human personality is made up of
a specific number of inborn mental "faculties"' each lo-
calized in a particular part of the brain, so that the relative size of the different cranial regions provided an index
of the strength of the particular faculty governed by that
area.

The idea of a relationship between head shape and
character has a long history, but it was most thoroughly
systematized as a "science" at the beginning of the last
century by two German physicians, Franz Joseph Gall
(1758–1828) and his student and collaborator, Johann
Kaspar Spurzheim (1776–1832). The system, as finally
developed by Spurzheim, recognized thirty-five distinct
faculties, divided into the two great classes of "Feelings"
and "Intellective Faculties." They were ordered thus:

FEELINGS:

Propensities or Impulses
    1. Amativeness. 2. Philoprogenitiveness. 3. Concentra-
tiveness. 4. Adhesiveness. 5. Combativeness. 6. Destruc-
tiveness. 6a. Alimentiveness. 7. Secretiveness. 8. Acquisi-
tiveness. 9. Constructiveness.

Sentiments: Lower (shared with lower animals)
    10. Self-esteem. 11. Love of Approbation. 12. Cautious-
ness.

Sentiments: Higher (peculiar to man)
    13. Benevolence. 14. Veneration. 15. Conscientiousness.

16. Firmness. 17. Hopefulness. 18. Wonder. 19. Ideality.
20. Wit. 21. Imitation.

INTELLECTIVE FACULTIES:

Perceptive Faculties
22. Individuality. 23. Form. 24. Size. 25. Weight. 26.
Color. 27. Locality. 28. Number. 29. Order. 30. Eventuality. 31. Time. 32. Tune. 33. Language.

Reflective Faculties
34. Comparison. 35. Causality.

Phrenology was not a fad limited to the gullible. Its
devotees included such people as Alfred Russel Wallace,
codiscoverer with Charles Darwin of the theory of evolution through natural selection; Arthur Conan Doyle,
creator of Sherlock Holmes; and the great American
poet Walt Whitman. Wallace and Doyle were also spiritualists—which makes one wonder whether there is a special faculty for being gullible, even among outstanding
people. There were always, to be sure, many doubters.
Gall and Spurzheim in 1808 presented a memoir on their
discoveries to the Institut de France, and a committee of
that august body drew up an unfavorable report. But institutes and academies have often rejected ideas that later
turned out to be fruitful.

I see no evidence that either Gall or Spurzheim should
be labeled "phony." They seem to have shared an ardent
belief in the importance and usefulness of their theories.
Whether or not they should be called "crackpot" is another matter. Advances in the knowledge of brain anatomy and function have shown that their ideas are entirely
untenable; but this has often happened in the course of
the history of ideas. I suppose that a crackpot is a person
who holds tenaciously to his ideas despite overwhelming
evidence against them, and it is difficult now to determine

the weight of the evidence in 1800. Many of the phrenologists who traveled through Europe and America earning their living by giving character sketches of their clients while feeling their heads undoubtedly were charlatans, shrewdly telling their clients what they most wanted to hear: but every profession has its charlatan fringe.

Phrenology has faded from the scene, but other crackpot methods of diagnosing personality are still very much with us. Palmistry, for instance. The world seems to be full of people able and willing to read one's character— and foretell the future—from the lines on the palms of the hands. Palmistry has a very long history, going back to the Egyptians, Assyrians, Greeks and Romans. When a subject has such a long and persisting history, one is tempted to wonder whether there may not be something to it. On the other hand, man clearly has an enormous capacity for being credulous and for continuing to believe things that are demonstrably untrue. If the antiquity and persistence of a belief were evidence of its validity, few things would be better attested than the existence of witches.

Human hands certainly differ greatly, certainly can be expressive; and it may well be that they could serve as an index to personality. Charlotte Wolff, a Polish physician and psychologist who worked at the University of London after the Nazi occupation of her country, has tried hard to demonstrate this idea, especially in a book called *The Human Hand*. She regards the hand as "a visible part of the brain," and I think there can be no question of her sincerity, or of her ability to judge character by an examination of hands—conditions of nails and fingers as well as of the lines of the palm. But I cannot see that she has come up with any very workable system.

Perhaps orthodox psychologists have shied away from any attempt to make scientific studies of hand characteristics because of the long history of charlatanism connected with the subject. The study of hypnosis was thus long neglected because it had acquired crackpot associations from the work of the German physician Franz Mesmer, and the cult of mesmerism developed in his name.

Reading character from the hands is sometimes called "chirosophy," to distinguish it from "chiromancy," reading the future from the lines of the palm. (The Chinese have an art of "pedomancy," reading the future from the feet.) For the validity of chiromancy there is no evidence whatever, yet the subject continues to flourish—sometimes as an amusing party game, but sometimes seriously. It is a human trait to want to peer into the future, and any system will be believed if clothed with enough ceremonial hocus-pocus: tea leaves, animal entrails, playing cards, crystal balls and the courses of the stars.

The persistence of astrology into the modern world is particularly puzzling. All literate people must now have some conception of the astronomical universe, realize that our earth is a rather minor planet circling a trivial star in one of many galaxies. How then could the movements of the stars, lost in the vast impersonal spaces of the universe, govern the fate of an individual, a cause, or a nation? Yet astrology continues to be a flourishing business.

The French are supposed to be a practical sort of people. Yet in the issue of *Time* Magazine for January 15, 1965 (and *Time* dotes on statistical accuracy) there is a report that "58% of all Frenchmen could say under what sign of the zodiac they had been born, 53% regularly read their daily horoscopes in the press, 43% thought of astrologers as scientists, 38% intended to have their horoscopes drawn up by an astrologer, and 37% believed that character traits correspond to zodiacal signs." The same article reports that "in Paris alone, there is one charlatan for every 120 Parisians, compared with one doctor for every 514 citizens and one priest for every 5,000."

Which raises the difficult question, what is a charlatan? Obviously, a person pretending to a knowledge or skill that he does not really possess. These are the phonies. A crackpot, on the other hand, sincerely believes in himself and in his cure for the ills of the world, however misguided he may seem to the rest of us. The distinction is not always easy to establish. Certainly there are many con men in the world, swindlers who know that they are selling widows worthless stocks or otherwise trading on the gullibility of mankind. But man's capacity for self-deception is also enormous, and many of the people with cures for cancer, or formulas for long life, or methods for predicting the future, undoubtedly believe in their own ideas, however crazy they may be. These crackpots, I suspect, cause far more damage than the phonies: a phony can always be exposed and deflated; but there is nothing that can be done about a crackpot except to shut him up, and who is to decide?

I think there is something of the phony in all of us: that we are all at times given to pretensions, and that at times we act in accord with expediency instead of conviction. Partly this is a question of manners: a person who tries always to be completely honest is apt to be pretty dreadful to have around. And a certain amount of phoniness may be necessary for success in public life—though many of our public figures seem to carry this to extremes.

An interesting case is that of the great violinist Fritz Kreisler, who confessed in February 1935 that he had been playing his own compositions for thirty years, but ascribing them to such early masters as Vivaldi, Couperin, Porpora, Pugnani and Padre Martini, saying that he had discovered the manuscripts in the course of his travels. That Kreisler felt the need for such a hoax illustrates nicely the difficulties in the path of the aspiring concert musician. As the Philadelphia *Record* commented, "We like to think of the composer as a man high above sordid earthly cares and of a virtuoso as one who has no thought for anything except his music. The glimpse here given of the maneuvering and strategy sometimes demanded by the divine art will comfort realtors, morticians and bond salesmen."

But the list of forgeries and hoaxes in the arts is a long one. Faking is more difficult in science because of the tradition of open work and the elaborate system of checking methods, experiments and ideas. Nevertheless frauds do occur. Perhaps the most famous case is that of Piltdown man. In 1908 a British lawyer and archaeologist, Charles Dawson, discovered a fragment of a human skull in a gravel pit near Piltdown, in southeastern England. Three years later he found another fragment. He took the bones to Sir Arthur Smith Woodward, the geologist of the British Museum. Sir Arthur thought Dawson might have found parts of a peculiar human fossil. The two of them continued to search the pits, and presently turned up part of an ape-like lower jaw which they assumed to belong with the cranial fragments. The discovery was announced in 1912, Sir Arthur naming the fossil *Eoanthropus dawsoni*. A good part of the scientific world never would believe that the ape-like jaw and man-like skull could have come from the same animal, but no one suspected fraud. Then in 1953, the British archaeologist Kenneth Oakley and his associates, while attempting to date the fossils by chemical analysis of their fluorine content, discovered that the jaw fragment was no fossil at all, but a bone from a modern ape carefully treated to give it an ancient appearance. The circumstances of the fraud remain obscure, but both Woodward and Dawson got their names in all of the anthropology books over a period of thirty years. Their names still appear in the books—though now in a different context.

Fraud however is rampant in the pseudosciences; here also the sincere crackpot has a wide scope for action, and distinguishing the crank from the scientist may be very difficult indeed. Martin Gardner, in a book on *Fads and Fallacies in the Name of Science,* lists five criteria for recognizing the paranoid pseudoscientist: (1) "He considers himself a genius." (2) "He regards his colleagues, without exception, as ignorant blockheads. Everyone is out of step except himself." (3) "He believes himself unjustly persecuted and discriminated against." (4) "He has strong compulsions to focus his attacks on the greatest scientists and the best-established theories." (5) "He often has a tendency to write in a complex jargon, in many cases making use of terms and phrases he himself has coined."

The pseudoscientific phonies and crackpots in our civilization have a tendency to concentrate on food and sex, perhaps because these are two areas in which our conventional culture is particularly vulnerable. They are also topics in which it is particularly difficult to distinguish fact from fiction and where it is hardly possible to carry out scientific experiments with the human animal—and where generalizations based on rats may well not apply to men. In both areas today's scientific orthodoxy may be tomorrow's aberration. I think of the attitude of all of the proper authorities of Victorian times toward masturbation: a horror leading to debility, insanity and goodness knows what else. Psychologists today are shocked at the probable damage caused by Victorian orthodoxy; does this make the Victorians crackpot?

It is as difficult, I suspect, to be really rational about nutrition as it is about sex. My doubts about the "science" of nutrition started back in the days of World War II when I was running a yellow fever laboratory in South America, where we maintained a considerable variety of laboratory animals. We feared that supplies of standard materials like cod-liver oil and wheat germ, used in our diets, might be cut off; so I began to explore the possibility of building up diets entirely with materials available locally. I found myself involved in a fascinating and complex series of experiments: shuffling kinds and proportions of materials much as in a prolonged card game. We managed to work out fairly satisfactory diets, though we never had to depend entirely on local materials; but what impressed me was that a diet satisfactory for one species of South American rodent would not necessarily be adequate for another species with apparently similar habits. If each kind of rat had its special requirements, how could one generalize from rats to people? For many kinds of nutritional studies we have to depend on laboratory animals. I don't object to this; but I do object to the positive statements based on such work. It sometimes seems to me that there are hardly any positive statements that can be made about human nutrition: but this doesn't stop the dietitians from sounding off; and they can sound just as prejudiced as the cranks and faddists.

Of food faddists there are no end—and the most diverse kinds seem to manage to get enough to eat. The vegetarians have clearly proven that man can get along without meat; while Vilhjalmur Stefansson and the Eskimos have also shown that he can get along without vegetables. There is an interminable list of food materials alleged to have special virtues—things like yogurt, blackstrap molasses, wheat germ, honey, sunflower seeds. It is easy to ridicule such foods, but some may well have special virtues; and even if they don't, the eater who thinks they do may get benefit through some obscure psychological channel. At least the food faddists often seem healthy and happy enough, despite the awful things they sometimes eat.

Food faddism is particularly rampant in the United States because of the national preoccupation with diets. We are undoubtedly the fattest nation in history. As S P R Charter has remarked in his book *Man on Earth,* "A fantastic percentage of wealth is devoted to fattening people, and an equally fantastic percentage of wealth is devoted to slimming them down again." Peter Wyden, in a book on *The Overweight Society,* reports a poll taken in 1964 which found that some 9.5 million Americans were on diets, while 16.4 million stated that they were watching their weight, and another 26.1 million expressed concern about their waistlines. This adds up to fifty-two millions consciously concerned with weight, and it is anyone's guess how many more should be concerned. This makes a splendid population for the operation of crackpots and phonies as well as serious-minded dietitians and psychologists—all of them apparently doing well.

There is the question not only of the quantity of food, but of its quality. And here the distinctions between science and pseudoscience become really confused. Martin Gardner, in a chapter on "Food Faddists," takes some sideswipes at "organic gardening" which seem to me at least to be misleading—propaganda for the chemical fertilizer people. Some of the claims of the organic gardeners may be pretty far-fetched; but the dangers of our increasing dependence on completely synthetic products are also real. One can get the other side of the picture from a sober book like Lewis Herber's *Our Synthetic Environment.* The chemistry of soil and the chemistry of nutrition are both complex and any simple explanation of the processes is apt to be wrong. Gardner, in the course of refuting the fallacy of organic farming, writes, "Soil and nutrition experts tell us that if plants grow at all, their composition tends to remain essentially the same, with respect to mineral and vitamin content, as plants grown in 'rich' soil." Herber, on the other hand, states, "The possibility of producing plants that 'look all right' but vary widely in nutritional values is more than theoretical; such cultivation is eminently practical and very common. Identical varieties of vegetables, fruit and grain may differ appreciably in mineral, protein and vitamin content." And Herber cites eminent and respected agricultural authorities in support of his point.

I don't want to get off into a discussion of gardening methods: I intend to continue using organic materials as well as synthetic fertilizers in my own garden—but I want to underline the difficulty of deciding what is crackpot in this area. I am sure that the insecticide manufacturers considered the late Rachel Carson crackpot after the publication of her book *Silent Spring;* and she undeniably—though necessarily—did overdramatize her case, to get needed attention. Her case however was clear and strong and very carefully documented: none of Martin Gardner's criteria for the paranoid crackpot could be applied. The manufacturers become suspect, square as they may seem in terms of the values of our society. Carelessness about harm to the consumer or to the environment seems to be built into our system, applying to drugs, detergents, automobiles—to all sorts of things, including the giant food industry. There is thus great need for criticism and control, as well as ample room for dissident opinion, crackpot or otherwise.

Sex has not yet been industrialized, though the contraceptive manufacturers are making progress—and of course the advertising boys depend on sex for selling almost everything else. I have no statistics, but I suspect that books about food and about sex are about equally numerous, and about equally difficult to evaluate. I suppose cookbooks are really more abundant than sex manuals—guides to a happy and well-adjusted sex life. But the how-to-do-it sex books are numerous enough, which is interesting because the variety of materials contributing to food is infinitely greater than the variety contributing to sex. The sex books have to rehash the same old stuff over and over. One wonders what would happen if cookbooks were subject to censorship and if many families felt that they had to hide *Fannie Farmer* (instead of *Fanny Hill*) from the children. The kids might at least take up cooking with more enthusiasm than most of them do at present.

Special theories about food are often tied up with religion: the vegetarianism of the Hindus, and among Christians, of the Seventh-Day Adventists, and all the special food taboos mentioned in an earlier chapter. Unconventional ideas about sex are also often justified on religious grounds. The polygamy of the early Mormons—definitely crackpot and downright immoral from the point of view of the surrounding society—was so justified, as were the sex habits of a number of other religious communities of the nineteenth century.

One of the most interesting of these was the Oneida Community founded by John Humphrey Noyes. The idea was that every member of the community should love every other member equally, and that marital fidelity was a sin of selfishness. Children however were only permitted to carefully chosen people, and were raised by the community to promote equality and to avoid what Noyes called the "idolatrous love of mother and child." Birth control was achieved by the method now called coitus reservatus, by which the man, during intercourse, manages to suppress ejaculation. Young men were initiated into this art by the older women of the colony, and girls by the older men. It all sounds very sensible to me. Yet in terms of our society, it was—and is—a crackpot idea. I am left with the feeling that what is crackpot, like what is phony, must be relative to the norms of the culture. This makes the squares—those who conform to social expectations—relative too.

It often seems to me that life is a sort of tightrope act, a matter of delicate balance between revolt and conformity. I don't want to act and sound different enough to be dismissed as a crackpot: it must be very lonely to be completely out of accord with society, to have few or none whom you can respect listen to your best ideas. On the other side, I don't want to fall into the pit of conformity. Life there may look comfortable enough—all those nice people always doing what they are supposed to do—but I suspect that for many there is a considerable cost in anxiety and frustration, breaking out sometimes in the form of ulcers or nervous breakdowns or nasty episodes in the divorce court.

If everyone conformed, culture (in the anthropological sense) would stagnate. I am not sure about our ideal of endless progress, but I do think there is ample room for improvement in our ideas and in our way of life. With change, however slow, there is always hope that it will be for the better—however that is to be measured. And if no one ever acted or thought unconventionally, there could be no change. But there is that tightrope again. You have to balance carefully, or the cops will get you.

XIII ❧ *Priests and Policemen*

> This unfortunate world has been blasted in all ages by two evil principles—Kingcraft and Priestcraft—that, taking advantage of two human necessities, in themselves not hard—salutary, and even beneficial in their natural operation—the necessity of civil government, and that of spiritual instruction, have warped them cruelly from their own pure direction, and converted them into the most odious, the most terrible and disastrous scourges of our race.
>
> WILLIAM HOWITT,
> *History of Priestcraft*
> *In All Ages and Nations*

TOM PAINE remarked somewhere that society was created because of man's needs; government, because of his wickedness. Which, if true, means that man must be pretty wicked, and growing wickeder all the time. Yet there seems to be no way of avoiding government—of avoiding social control of individual behavior. As people multiply, becoming ever more crowded, and as technologies become ever more complex and potentially dangerous, the need for regulation becomes ever greater.

There are, of course, the anarchists, who hopefully believe that government can be abolished; but, as a movement, they have been very quiet lately. Perhaps the monstrous growth of government everywhere discourages even the most starry-eyed philosopher; perhaps the failure of practicing communism to lead to any detectable diminution of governmental control has also been discouraging —though the philosophies of anarchism and communism have had separate histories and goals. At any rate, I have heard of few contemporary believing anarchists, though I know a number of people (including myself) who find the theory attractive.

Prince Kropotkin, an influential anarchist philosopher around the turn of the century, summarized the idea in his article in the eleventh edition of the *Encyclopaedia Britannica* thus: "*Anarchism,* the name given to a principle or theory of life and conduct under which society is conceived without government . . . harmony in such a society being obtained, not by submission to law, or by obedience to any authority, but by free agreements concluded between various groups, territorial and professional, freely constituted for the sake of production and consumption, as also for the satisfaction of the infinite variety of needs and aspirations of a civilized being." A nice idea, isn't it? But we will probably never know whether or not it would work, because it never will be tried—though some lessening of conflict among authorities would seem to be necessary if civilization is to survive.

The entanglement of the anarchist movement with violence toward the end of the nineteenth century is a complex story, tied up with the struggle of labor for recognition and rights. The connection in the public mind is unfortunate, because anarchist philosophy is essentially nonviolent. Prince Kropotkin, who started out as a biologist, made a considerable contribution to evolutionary theory by emphasizing the cooperative aspects of nature, which tend to get lost in a misleading concentration on the competitive "struggle for existence."

But we are concerned here not so much with things as

they might be as with things as they are; and governments, along with a variety of military and police organizations for enforcing their will, are very much a present reality. So are religions. Church and state are supposed to be separate, but it is not always easy to distinguish between religion and government. Nationalism sometimes strikes me as a religion—of a particularly vicious sort in a shrinking world where there is no longer room for intolerance and misunderstanding. There is something idolatrous about the worship of a flag; and treason becomes hard to distinguish from heresy.

Curiously, it is hard to define any of the words I have been using—government, religion, law and the like—and I am not even going to try. My interest is in the social control of individual behavior, the array of commands and prohibitions that govern the conduct of all of us. In our civilization it seems to me that these fall into three broad classes: custom, civil law and spiritual regulation. Customary behavior is governed by public opinion; civil law by police and courts; religious observance by the priesthood.

The distinctions, of course, are far from clear. Law supposedly reflects custom—and customs sometimes are incorporated into legal codes, sometimes not. Sexual behavior seems to me a matter of custom, but in our culture what is presumed to be majority practice is often spelled out in laws. Food behavior, on the other hand, is mostly left to control by neighborly opinion. There is no law about three meals a day or about which fork to use for the salad, though there are plenty of laws about the sale and distribution of foods. Civil law and spiritual regulation also get all mixed up: witness the Sunday blue laws. And it is often hard to distinguish between local custom and religious observance: if customs don't become laws, they may well become religious rites. Which all adds up to the easy observation that civilized life is complicated, and not made any simpler by the welter of controls. How did we get this way?

Any animal society needs a set of habits or instincts that will hold the group together and some method of determining the nature of group action. From the point of view of the possible origins of human social behavior, the most interesting societies are those of mammals, and especially of monkeys and apes. They have been the subject of a number of careful studies in recent years, which I have drawn on at various points in this book. Coordination within the group is achieved chiefly through the establishment of a dominance hierarchy, or peck order—but this takes a variety of forms. With the howler monkeys of Panama dominance seems to be entirely absent, the lead sometimes taken by one animal, sometimes by another. With baboons, cliques develop within the larger social group; and leadership and discipline fall to a few elderly males who generally stick together. With gorillas there is a single "Old Man" who might be considered the dictator, or chief, but his rule is benign indeed. Human tribal chieftainship may well have had its origins in a behavior pattern like that of the gorillas. But with the development of culture and of language, things must have rapidly become complicated.

Social control must at first have been a matter of custom: the elders teaching the younger generation the traditional ways of doing things. Learning in man doesn't seem to differ greatly from learning in other animals: his uniqueness is in the great development of teaching. Look at the tricks we can teach a dog, a chimpanzee, a seal or an elephant, but which they in turn cannot pass on. And some of the things we teach one another or our children are probably just as absurd as the tricks we teach our pets.

Custom in a small group can be a very powerful social control. Deviant behavior—doing things differently—is almost unthinkable; and since everyone knows all about everyone else, conformity is almost necessarily complete. Custom would early govern not only behavior among individuals, but behavior in relation to the world around —animals, plants, rocks, storms. Spirits must also soon have formed part of this world; animate, inanimate, natural, supernatural would hardly be distinguished. Practices that we would class as magic governed relations with the external world, and my distinction between custom and religious regulation would be quite meaningless in Stone Age or Neolithic societies.

With the emergence of specialists in magic and specialists in knowledge of the needs and behavior of spirits and gods, we have the beginnings of the priesthood, of specialists in knowledge of how people ought to act. But there would still be no way of separating civil and religious. At the beginning of historic times we find priest and king sometimes identical, sometimes interchangeable, sometimes separate—but generally in accord about the management of human affairs. Caesar and God had the same interests.

Social control began to be difficult with the development of cities, city-states—and empires. Custom could not be depended on in a crowded city, where everyone no longer knew everyone else and where specialization in crafts and professions created problems in the distribution of goods and inequalities in wealth and status. The idea of "property" evolved, and has been plaguing us ever since. It was found necessary to write out the rules, especially those governing property and personal safety—which resulted in the development of law. The priests, who invented writing in response to the need of keeping track of the increasingly complex affairs of the temples, also found it expedient to write out the rules governing relationships with the gods.

I am greatly oversimplifying in my effort to sketch some

background for a look at social controls of behavior in the modern world. But an accurate history of social control would be difficult to write. We have an immense body of information about the laws of past times, since even some ancient codes have survived, but we know extraordinarily little about methods of law enforcement. The cops and their past equivalents, surely always important in determining the actions of men, get very little space in the history books. Our ignorance, and the neglected importance of police actions in shaping the course of history, are underlined in a book by Charles Reith, *The Blind Eye of History*, which has the subtitle "A study of the origins of the present Police Era."

The word "police" in the meaning of "the civil force to which is entrusted the duty of maintaining public order" is modern, gaining wide use only after 1829 when the police system of London was established by act of Parliament. The words for the various kinds of law-enforcing agencies tried in the past are as numerous as are the kinds of agencies—most of which, it seems, did not work very well. Life and property for the ordinary person have been pretty precarious throughout history—highwaymen, bandits, petty thieves and the like have abounded. Only the rich or powerful could gain some security with their armed servants and bodyguards.

In tribal societies, when custom is violated and damage caused to an individual or his property, punishment (or vengeance) is generally in the hands of the kin of the victim. This works because of the strong force of tribal opinion in condemning violation of custom, which provides support for the avenging kin. But this system breaks down with the crowding and social diversification of city formation. The Greeks nevertheless continued the tribal form of law enforcement in their city-states, making every citizen a policeman, responsible for arresting and bringing to court anyone found violating the law.

This "remarkable system of law enforcement machinery soon ceased to function effectively," Reith remarks, "but the Greeks clung to it and, strangely, could visualize no other. The Greeks did what can be seen to have been done in all communities in all ages to meet confusion caused by the weakness of law-enforcement machinery, when this is not recognized as being the cause of crime and confusion. They made more laws, and these inevitably increased confusion by increasing the strain on such means as already existed for securing law-observance."

Reith cites many other cases in which attempts to control disorder by passing laws have failed, and all of us can think of modern cases. The habit of attempting to solve a problem by passing a law seems to be deeply ingrained. The height of absurdity was reached in eighteenth-century England when crime became rampant with the breakdown of the parish-constable system, a consequence of the social changes brought on by the Industrial Revolution. Crimes punishable by hanging reached the number of 223—among them that of stealing from a person goods to the value of one shilling. Cartloads of people were driven to Tyburn every few weeks for public hanging, but crime continued to increase.

The problem of rampant crime in London was finally solved by the abandonment of the parish-constable idea and the creation of a wholly new police institution. This new institution, as Reith remarks, was built "fortuitously, unconsciously, without definite and detailed plan, except in the final, visible form of its production"—the usual British way of doing things. But the result, I think most people would agree, is the best police system in the world from the point of view of maintenance of order without tyranny. Reith gives most credit to the novelist Henry Fielding, who had the idea of building a police force for the prevention of crime, rather than for the punishment of crimes after they were committed.

The London police system was gradually extended to the boroughs and counties of the provinces in the first half of the nineteenth century, but with local autonomy. The Metropolitan Police of London (whose headquarters are Scotland Yard) are responsible to the Home Secretary, but he has no direct authority over the provincial police. Half the cost of each police force, however, is paid by the central government; and the Home Secretary can withhold the money if he finds that funds are not being spent wisely and effectively. There is thus real central control, though without the creation of a specific national ministry of police.

The United States must have about the most complex and confused collection of police systems of any modern state. There are more than forty thousand separate police forces: village, town, city, county and state. There are also eight independent federal groups with police functions, the most famous of which is the FBI—the Federal Bureau of Investigation. This does not take into account secret services like the Central Intelligence Agency and Naval Intelligence, though spying and policing frequently appear to be overlapping functions.

Governments and rulers throughout history have tried to use armies for police functions, but such attempts have invariably failed. There is something about the nature of an army that makes it unsuitable for policing civil populations. On the other hand, rulers have from early times found that an extension of their bodyguard system could make an efficient police organization, serving both their personal purposes and those of the state: individual liberty might not be protected, but order could be maintained. This is the origin of the centralized gendarmerie police of most modern nations. Mussolini and Hitler demonstrated nicely how such police systems could be used for gaining and maintaining power. Order certainly was imposed—but at a cost.

With such dictatorships the cost of the police system is clear; there can be no disagreement with official ideas or practices. But order always has a cost; there are always problems of balance between individual liberty and public good, sometimes quite obvious, but sometimes subtle. Often I think we have not tried to find the reasonable balance: we have become enamored of regulation for its own sake.

The problem of individual freedom versus social good is nicely posed in the case of public health measures, because the issues are least clouded by inherited prejudice and superstition; yet the proper course of action may be far from obvious. I saw the possible dilemma vividly some years ago in the course of a conference in the office of the governor of the Pacific island trust territory of Truk. A trade ship had gone off its scheduled route the night before to drop an anthropologist and me on the island so we could get an airplane to Guam. The governor asked us if we would be interested in attending his weekly staff conference next morning to see something of the administrative problems of the Territory.

Much of the conference was given over to discussion between the chief justice and the chief health officer. It appeared that the health officer had not allowed the crew or deck passengers of the ship ashore, though the ship had stayed in port all night. The American officers had been allowed to land, however, with us. The lawyer was indignant: how could we inculcate the principles of democracy in the face of such rank class or race discrimination? The health man, however, pointed out that after long and painstaking effort he had succeeded in eradicating venereal disease completely on the island; and he did not propose to see this careful work wrecked overnight by a group of natives from other islands. The freedom of the native passengers and crew was thus sacrificed for the social good of the island.

I don't know how one would determine the proper course in such a situation: perhaps everyone going ashore, including us, should have been required to submit to a physical examination. My sympathies, however, were more with the lawyer's point of view than with the physician's. There is no denying the benefits of modern public health practices in the protection of the community. The terror of epidemics has been removed from our catalogue of fears, and the people of the Western world live longer and healthier lives than any people ever have. The reduction in physical pain and misery is a tremendous gain; but it has costs. Someone has remarked that the public health ideal would be to have the whole population in jail, to ensure that everyone got the right diet, the proper immunizing shots, and so forth.

Often the costs are trivial, like not being allowed to spit in the subway. Then there are the nuisances like getting vaccination certificates before going abroad. But sometimes the cost to the individual is considerable: incarceration and isolation in the case of a contagious disease. The aim is to protect society, not to punish the individual—but the individual still suffers. I often think that our culture has gone to extremes in its fear of contagion. We see germs everywhere; they have become as powerful and as all-pervasive as the spirits of the primitive world. And the rituals of exorcism often seem equally irrational: we have replaced the bull-roarer with the gauze mask and stethoscope. But the relationship between witchcraft and modern medicine, fascinating though it is, is irrelevant here.

With contagious disease the situation is fairly clear. The epidemiology of disease has become a considerable science, and our knowledge is constantly increasing. The epidemiology of sin is quite another matter. We act as though we know all about it, attempting to immunize, to quarantine, to eradicate; but our methods are pretty much based on tradition. There is little reason or science involved in our actual practices, though we have a number of high-sounding words like penology and criminology.

What is sin, anyway? We define disease as a departure from a state of health. I suppose sin, in the very broad sense in which I have been using it, could be defined as a departure from a state of social conformity. The word also has a narrow meaning as a violation of religious or spiritual regulations. If we go back to the distinction I made at the beginning of this chapter, violation of civil law would be a crime. It is difficult to find a single word to cover violation of custom—but maybe eccentricity will do. This word is neutral enough to cover such things as growing a beard when beards are not fashionable, wearing the wrong clothes, collecting butterflies, and so on through various degrees of neurosis to the vague boundary that sets off the psychotic. We would thus have three broad classes of social deviants: sinners, criminals and oddballs.

One would think these would be easy enough to distinguish, so that sin could be handled by the priests, crime by the police and oddity by the neighbors. But in fact we seem to confuse the three easily, which makes the study of their epidemiology difficult. All three are, at least at times, regarded as contagious—leading to treatment analogous with the treatment of disease.

Communism makes a nice case. We apparently regard it as highly contagious: speakers with communist ideas are often barred from giving public lectures, apparently from fear of infection. We forbid or greatly restrict travel to certain communist countries and vice versa, with the idea of imposing quarantine. There are complications here, since Americans are now allowed to go to Russia, and Russians to come to the United States. But countries like Cuba and China are strictly barred, though I am not sure that there is any evidence of a special geographical virulence. Curiously, a Russian communist can visit the United States, but a British communist may find it very difficult to get a visa. Foreigners in general are given a detailed examination before being granted a visa, to be sure that there is no trace of subversive infection. In many communist countries, of course, capitalism gets the same treatment that communism does here.

Is communism a sin, a crime or an oddity? Our reaction is very like the reaction to heresy, which would make it a sin. And certainly it violates our most deeply held religious principles about both God and private property. But we pass laws about it so that it becomes a crime. To me, in the social environment of the United States, it seems merely an oddity like beards or vegetarianism.

So many people of my generation were either party members or sympathizers during the 1930s that I have often wondered how I escaped infection. My analysis is fairly simple. I could never take Hegel, and since Marxian theory is based on Hegelian dialectic, I was protected from the beginning. I wonder whether large doses of Hegel would serve for general immunization. The trouble is that Hegel, in some people, produces no negative reaction—they may even like his philosophy. I suppose the only thing one can do with such people is to let the ideological infection take its course; at least jails and truncheons don't seem to be good therapy, and there are sometimes spontaneous recoveries.

There is a complication in the epidemiology of communism and of many other sins and crimes—the missionary syndrome. A convinced communist wants to convert as many people as he can to his ideas, so perhaps we should speak of fear of conversion rather than fear of contagion. We think of missionary work as an attribute of religion, but that is because of our Christian background. Most religions have been expressions of the outlook of a particular people, and where religions have spread, it has been through military conquest or cultural contact. But Christianity, Buddhism and Islam have all, at one time or another, set out to save the world, each after its own fashion. Christianity, since the days of Saint Paul, has been particularly dedicated to missionary activity; and in modern times Americans have taken up missionary work with especial zeal. According to the *Encyclopedia Americana* two-thirds of the thirty-four thousand Protestant foreign missionaries working in 1956 were Americans, as were many of the Catholic missionaries.

There is nothing much that can be done about a missionary: he is so sure he is right, and so eager to save other people. The missionary syndrome reaches its greatest development among Christians and communists, but it can be found in all sorts of other activities. I suppose I am following a missionary impulse in writing this book, trying to make converts to ideas that appeal to me: there is something of the missionary in all of us.

The missionary syndrome becomes particularly difficult with religion because of its involvement with the priest complex. I am using "priest" in the sense of the first definition in the Oxford English Dictionary: "One whose office is to perform public religious functions; an official minister of religious worship." Protestant clergymen, in this sense, are priests, however much they may dislike the label. The word "priest," of course, was associated with the Roman Church at the time of the Reformation, and the word was discarded along with the theology. William Howitt, from whose book on the evils of priestcraft comes the quotation at the head of this chapter, was a devout Quaker; about a third of his book is devoted to the tyranny of priests of pagan religions, the rest to the Roman Church, with a few blasts toward the end at the English Church. The Quakers have probably freed themselves as completely as possible from priestly activities; but Protestants in general, in eliminating the word, hardly succeeded in eliminating the function. Protestant ministers, when they have had the power, have sometimes been as arbitrary, rigid and dictatorial as the priests of any religion.

The difficulty with the priest complex is that, in its fullest development, it confers on the bearer a sort of omniscience which, when combined with missionary zeal, can lead to all sorts of untoward consequences. The extension of spiritual regulation to nonspiritual aspects of life—food, sex, clothing, manners, daily routines—ordinarily represents a sort of codification of tribal or local custom which may or may not be appropriate in other situations. Thus we have the oft-cited case of missionaries getting clothes on the South Sea Islanders in a climate where any clothing is inappropriate or even harmful; but there may also be more subtle deleterious changes. I remember noticing in Micronesia that on Christianized islands, the natives had been taught to hide in the bushes to defecate, while the original custom was to use the lagoon. There are no human intestinal parasites that can complete their life cycles in salt water, so the original custom was extremely sanitary. The Western custom can be made sanitary with outhouses, bored-hole latrines and the like—but how much more complex! And what does this have to do with spiritual regulation?

A Catholic priest on one of the islands who was trying to make converts with a minimum disruption of local customs told me that there was nothing in Christian doctrine that required interment of the dead. Yet many missionaries seem to think that a graveyard is an essential adjunct of a church, thus on tiny islands removing needed land from use. The indigenous custom of burying the dead at sea would seem much more reasonable.

The separation of civil and religious institutions has now come to be recognized almost everywhere, at least in official documents. Therefore missionaries generally must operate through changes in custom rather than changes in law—except in the control of such pagan behavior as cannibalism and polygamy. They have to persuade people that the missionary way of doing things is the right way—a process of conversion rather than contagion or compulsion. This is sometimes difficult. It is, for instance, very rare for a Mohammedan to become converted to Christianity, and I have been told that Islam is the fastest-spreading religion in the world today.

The struggle to remove from the priesthood the power of inflicting physical punishment has been a long one. A catalogue of the meannesses inflicted by man on man in the name of religion, like that garnered by William Howitt in his *History of Priestcraft,* makes a dismal record, much of it too well documented to be explained away: the mad sacrifices of the Aztecs, the enslaving caste system of the Hindus, the fanatic excesses of the Spanish Inquisition. Howitt quotes statistics from the records of the Inquisition: 31,912 burned at the stake, 291,450 condemned to severe penances. And this must be a trivial percentage of the number of people who have been killed in the name of Christianity if all of the wars, crusades and persecutions are added up. It can't happen any more, one thinks. We have made moral progress. But then comes the memory of Nazi Germany.

Where is Utopia?

XIV ❧ Toward Utopia

> Now tidiness is undeniably a good—but a good of which it is easily possible to have too much and at too high a price. . . . The good life can be lived only in a society where tidiness is preached and practiced, but not too fanatically, and where efficiency is always haloed, as it were, by a tolerated aura of mess.
>
> ALDOUS HUXLEY,
> *Themes and Variations*

EACH SEMESTER I have a seminar that meets one evening a week at my house. This gives me a chance to get acquainted with a dozen or so students from different parts of the university—one of my rules is, no more than two students from a particular department. We pick some topic of general interest and spend the semester reading and talking about it: another rule is that the topic be something I don't know much about, so that I can't sound off in the usual professorial manner. I really think that students learn most when the teacher doesn't know any more than they do, because then they have to dig things out for themselves. (This, of course, would not apply to training in skills.) Anyway, the seminar is arranged for my benefit, rather than that of the students; and I have learned a great deal from it over the years.

One semester we picked Utopia as the topic. Everyone complains so much about the defects of the world we live in—and this is especially true of bright students—that I thought it would be easy to design a better one. We read and discussed a whole series of utopian books, from Plato's *Republic* to B. F. Skinner's *Walden Two*.

To my surprise, we got nowhere. We could think of all sorts of ways in which present laws should be liberalized, police methods improved, education reformed, international understanding promoted; but we arrived at no basic restructuring of society. Furthermore, we had no desire to live in any of the utopias we read about; they all seemed pretty dull.

Our basic trouble, we decided, was that we could not arrive at any clear statement of the purpose of society—the purpose of living. Purpose, we realized, is a very tricky concept, one that often causes trouble when it gets introduced into a discussion. It is probably purely a construct of the human mind: there is no purpose in nature. But as humans we are always looking for purposes, and we are much happier when we think we have found one. It was really difficult to think about the organization of society, without some idea of what it was organized for. After months of discussion, the best we could come up with was Life, Liberty and the pursuit of Happiness—which was not very original. But I still have not been able to think of a better statement of purpose.

Life. The whole system of nature seems to be arranged to insure the continuity of the life process. The individual struggles to survive, but may be sacrificed to promote the continuity of the population, of the species. Species in turn become extinct, but their role in the community is carried on by some new species. As George Gaylord Simpson has noted, evolution can be looked at as a relay race, with particular roles passed from species to species through geological time; the continuity is that of the biological community.

There is, to be sure, a great deal of killing in nature.

As I have remarked, the biological community is organized in terms of who eats whom. But the killing is governed by a complex set of checks and balances. In particular, the reproductive rate of any species is related to the hazards of existence for that species: oysters have an immense reproductive potential, elephants a very low one. Man's killing, insofar as it is a product of his culture rather than his biology, is quite outside this system, which is why his activities have led to the disappearance of so many other forms of life.

But man's habit of killing other men is particularly absurd. It is, as I have tried to point out, a cultural development, and some cultural method of control must be developed if our species and our civilization are to survive.

Liberty. This is more difficult, and biology is of little help. Except that to me the great significance of the human experience lies in the possibility of freedom for the individual. Many organisms have solved the problems of totalitarian social organization. I cannot see anything biologically interesting about human society as an ant hill—or sociologically interesting either. But my attitude is a consequence of my intellectual heritage; and when I start out to justify it, I am probably rationalizing rather than reasoning. It is, I am afraid, a belief: that the individual should be as free as is possible so long as he doesn't damage others or the social group.

That is the problem: defining the limits on liberty. I think people should be allowed to get drunk if they want to. But what about driving an automobile while drunk? And is drunkenness any excuse for beating up your wife? And how do we arrive at the proposition that it is wrong to take a drink until your twenty-first birthday has arrived? Why is it all right to smoke tobacco, but not marijuana? Why for that matter is it wrong to take heroin? Clearly there is damage; but it is damage to the individual. How far should we go in protecting people from themselves? I suppose the idea of contagion comes up here again. If people are allowed to take drugs if they want to—fully advised of the dangers—many people will acquire the habit and society will be damaged. But I am not sure that we know much about the contagiousness of habits: the epidemiology of sin is a neglected study.

Happiness. Here we get into real trouble. "Happiness is a warm puppy" is probably as good a definition as any. At that seminar we finally decided we were all hedonists. We found that one trouble with utopia was that there wouldn't be anything to gripe about. And how can you be happy without gripes? In the present world, at least, there is plenty of room for complaint.

Sometimes I think we complain too much. When I look back over history, I cannot think of any previous age in which I would want to live, unless I could specify such circumstances as social class. Fifth-century Athens sounds exciting, but not for the slaves; Elizabethan England— but again, for a few lucky souls. Today I wouldn't want to have to make my way out of a Southern sharecropper background, or out of the slums of one of our great cities. The struggle for racial equality and for equality of opportunity sometimes seems interminable. But in the Western world, at least, a greater proportion of people have a chance of leading satisfying lives than at any time in the past, even though there is still a long way to go before reaching any utopian ideal.

We fuss about the pressures for conformity, about the effect of the mass media in creating a mass culture. We ought to fuss, certainly: those rows of little boxes in suburbia are depressing; and the picture of America as God's own junkyard is altogether too valid. But when I look for reassurance, I reflect that the pressures today are less than they were fifty years ago, and I think I can find evidence that this is a continuing trend, that there is an increasing diversity of styles of life open to the individual. As for the little boxes: even the builders are beginning to be ashamed of themselves, and there are signs that we are entering a period of more rational city and regional planning, though I must admit it is hard to find reassurance in those monotonous new throughways.

I suppose this whole book is a plea for tolerance of diversity. Diversity seems to me a good in itself. I can justify this in biological terms: the most stable biological communities are those with the greatest variety of organisms. Diversity means that if something happens to one kind of animal or plant, others are present to take over; there is a great deal of "play" in the system. If elms were a tropical forest tree, for instance, the Dutch elm disease would not be much of a tragedy because of the hundreds of other kinds of trees. The same argument applies to human economy: the more diversified the economy, the safer it is from disaster because of accidents to one crop or one industry.

The leap from economics to esthetics is a large one: from diversity in industry to diversity in styles of life. Yet variety always gives a wide range of materials from which to build toward the future: variety in the biological community for the working of evolution; variety in the economy for national wealth; and shall I say variety in the ways of living for the realization of happiness? Probably satisfactions would be a better word. Different possibilities in the wearing of clothes, in the design of houses, in the kinds of work, in ways of finding recreation, in eating food. And sex?

I started this book with the idea that food and sex were biologically comparable drives; but that food in our culture was relatively neutral, relatively free from warping by traditional prejudice; whereas sex, particularly with the Christian heritage, has come under strong control by custom, by law, and by religion. We might, I thought, gain some insight on sex by looking at food.

I am not at all sure this is true, even after writing a book on it: whether the argument for diversity in food can be carried over to sex. After all, food and sex *are* different. The maintenance of the individual depends on the one, the continuation of the species on the other. And with man, sex is deeply involved with the institution of the family. I am not going to go out shouting in behalf of motherhood, but I will put in a mild plug for the family; it has worked quite well for a long time, and none of the utopian schemes for doing away with it has been adequately tested. Many of our attitudes about the family, however, seem to me cultural rather than biological, and consequently subject to cultural modification. I even suspect that sexual jealousy may be culturally learned, in view of the recent observations on the absence of such jealousy in chimpanzees and gorillas, and in view of the variety of practices in different human societies.

The family system may in any event become modified by population developments. Richard Meier, in his book *Modern Science and the Human Fertility Problem,* discusses at some length the possibility that in the future a significant proportion of the population may lead perfectly happy, but nonreproductive, lives. He gives a list of "sterile professions" which in the past have been largely male occupations, but which could equally well be handled by women. Childlessness is particularly advantageous in the case of work involving geographical mobility, and Meier's list includes everything from fruit pickers and truckdrivers to diplomats and professional athletes. Meier suggests that special forms of marriage might be developed for members of these sterile professions. A companionate marriage, for instance, "recognized in law as a kind of limited liability partnership," which could be easily dissolved in the absence of complicating children. For sociable individuals he proposes a "complex family" unit, including "a multiplicity of adults and a few children." It sounds to me as though Meier also thought that sexual jealousy was culturally learned, at least if members of the complex family were going to share sex as well as food.

We are certainly making progress in the Western world in liberalizing attitudes toward sex, and this seems to me entirely good in view of all the miseries that the psychologists have revealed to us as being caused by sexual repressions—better, surely, than the duplicity of the Victorians. The dreadful aspect of unsanctioned sex has been the unwanted children—dreadful for mother, sometimes for father and almost always for the children. This, with modern contraception, need no longer occur if we can get the knowledge to those who should have it. There is, of course, all of the fuss about our deteriorating morals, juvenile delinquency and the other ills of our permissive society. I am not at all sure that our morals are deteriorating when I read about prostitution in the last century; and if delinquency is increasing, I suspect it has many causes other than changing sexual attitudes. As for permissiveness: I think we would do better to follow Crane Brinton's suggestion, toward the end of his *History of Western Morals*, that we should talk about a "more humanitarian society."

People, undeniably, are interesting. It is easy to be amused at the antics of the human animal: at his curious habit of trying to improve on nature by trimming his hair, putting on paint and wearing uncomfortable extra skins; at his finickiness about what is fit to eat and what isn't; at all of the prohibitions that hedge in the expression of sexual impulses; at his conceit and pretensions. It is also easy to be frightened by the power men have to be mean to one another, either singly or acting as political groups; by the dizzy way in which the number of people is multiplying so that presently, if the trend continues, there will be no room for anything except humanity on the planet; by the deterioration of the environment, the pollution of air and water, the reckless depletion of slowly accumulated resources. If one stops to look around, it is difficult to be optimistic about the future of our species.

There is, to be sure, the reassurance of accomplishment. We have done all sorts of extraordinary things with our machines; we have guided evolution to develop efficient crop plants and to turn cows and chickens into apparatuses for the production of milk and eggs; we have built cities and dams, altering the surface of our planet with unprecedented speed. And there is no reason to suppose that we have come anywhere near the limits of our inventiveness. We have achieved political systems which enable many millions of individuals to live together in peace, safety and comfort—though we are still far from solving the problem of reconciling divergent political systems.

And so one vacillates between hope for Utopia and fear for Dystopia—fear for the inverted or wrecked society that has become the theme of so much recent writing. But, for me, the hope has to win, we have to keep trying; otherwise the wreck becomes inevitable. And I can see no reason why the human experiment should fail—it has so many interesting possibilities.

I like the last chapter, an "Avowal of Optimism," in a recent book *On Aggression* by the eminent student of animal behavior Konrad Lorenz. He is hopeful that through more thorough study of animal behavior and wider diffusion of what we know, we will gain a better understanding of ourselves and find ways to discharge our aggressions with less damage than is the case at present. Aggressive behavior, certainly, is widespread in the animal kingdom, but only in man does it seem to be out of control. Faith in the possibility of learning through science is often dismissed as "scientism" and labeled as a curse of our age: but in reviewing the past and the damage caused by unscientific ideas, I can't accept this judgment. Not that I would want to put the government of the world in the hands of scientists: they are people, with all of the defects of other varieties of that species. It is scientific knowledge and scientific attitudes that I would like to see more widely dispersed.

Lorenz finds a number of other reasons for optimism: art, as much as science, can lead to international understanding, as can development of ways of promoting more acquaintance among differing peoples. But the point he makes that I particularly like, and that hadn't occurred to me before, concerns the importance of humor. Laughter is a peculiarly human characteristic. It is in all probability based in aggression. But laughter has become either, on the one hand, harmless, or on the other, extremely useful in deflating pomposity, in disclosing lies, in bringing out the most pleasant aspects of our species. And there is a bond among those who can share laughter. As Lorenz remarks, "Barking dogs may occasionally bite, but laughing men hardly ever shoot!"

Or as I sometimes put it, serious subjects should be treated lightly. I have been serious, but I have tried to be light. And so, to go back to the beginning, what is natural for man? Very little, as far as I can see. Culture has swamped biology. The human animal is there, somewhere, but so deeply encrusted with tradition, with ideas, with learned behavior, that he is hard to find. And what we call the beast in man is almost always the consequence of this encrustation: animal nature out of control because of the cultural overlay.

I sometimes speculate about how it all got started. It must have been way back at the beginning of the Pleistocene, when we first find tools that have obviously been shaped—and man is the animal that makes tools according to a predetermined design. I can imagine those protohominids, squatting around in their lair, and one of the young ones picking up a stone and chipping at it with another, making it sharper, more effective.

Language would have been very undeveloped then, and ideas nonexistent, since ideas depend on words. But I can still imagine the old fellows regarding this young one with great doubt. If they had had words to think with, their minds would have worked something like this: "Natural rocks were good enough for our ancestors, and they are good enough for us. We have no business interfering with nature—only harm can come."

And sometimes, when I look about me, I wonder.

❧ Notes and Sources

When I wrote an article entitled "Man, Food and Sex" for *The American Scholar* in 1958 (which, with some alteration, forms the second chapter of this book) I realized that the idea might well need a whole book for development. I toyed with this possibility for a couple of years, talking about it with anyone who would listen, and drawing up various outlines which I still have carefully filed away. My first plan was to make a geographical and historical survey of food habits, with only occasional reference to sexual analogies. I still think such a book could be interesting and informative. But then, I thought, why be serious? I have long had a not-very-secret desire to be a humorist—which has not been much encouraged by either editors or publishers. Food could be a fine way of ridiculing some of our attitudes toward sex, with sideswipes at psychology in general. Personality theory, for instance: fussy feeders, messy feeders, reluctant feeders and the like. Some of this remains in the present book—like the reference to food perversions. But book-length levity is not easily sustained.

The article in *The American Scholar* triggered a surprising number of letters with thoughtful ideas and comments. I remember particularly a letter from John R. Brobeck, M.D., of the Department of Physiology of the University of Pennsylvania, pointing out how generally our physiology is influenced by our ideas. "For example," he wrote, "we all breathe publicly; but dyspnea is 'indecent' unless it follows something like a footrace and even then, I suspect, it has its embarrassing elements." It was this letter that led me to think of expanding from the particular problems of food and sex to the general human problem of being natural. His letter, I note, was dated June 22, 1959.

In the years since then I have talked with many people; given lectures on food and sex, or on the human problem of being natural, in many colleges—the lectures always followed by thought-provoking discussions with bright and interested students. Under these circumstances, I couldn't possibly give proper credit for the sources of most of my ideas. I haven't tried except in the case of books or articles that might be of interest to people wanting to follow-up particular topics.

I owe, as always, a considerable debt to my agent, Diarmuid Russell, and my editors, Jason Epstein and Berenice Hoffman —not only for encouragement and suggestions, but for patience in waiting six years for a book that had been promised in two. Four student research assistants have got involved in helping me over this period: Howard Beemer, Keith Kellogg, Clifford Blankenship and Roger Wykes. They have all contributed their own ideas as well as garnering the ideas of other people from books in the library. Roger, among other things, typed the final draft of the manuscript, picking up many a slip on the way, so that any appearance of accuracy must be considered his fault as much as mine. William J. Thornton of the University of Michigan library staff has spent a great deal of time (when off duty) tracking down items for us in the complex University library system. Beyond this, my wife, my children, and many of my friends have read all or parts of the manuscript—after all, it has been lying around the house for several years. Which makes me wonder whether I should rephrase the usual statement, and ask that any mistakes be blamed on the suggestions of my friends.

As for bibliographic detail: it seems pedantic to repeat in these notes books or articles that have been cited by title and author in the text, unless some special qualification or elaboration seems needed. Author and title are enough to locate the book in a library card catalogue or for the bookseller to track it down. In the case of journal articles, I have tried to cite the year of publication consistently. Some residual scholarly infection, however, has led us to make more complete citations when the source for a fact or idea is first mentioned in these notes.

1. *On Being Human*

This chapter is based so largely on personal experience that documentation is hardly needed. Curiously, the problems of the elimination of body wastes, which get so much attention here, are hardly mentioned in the rest of the book; I suppose they could easily have formed a chapter. Public facilities for elimination seem particularly scarce in the United States, except for filling stations and bars. Roger Wykes, one of my student research assistants, suggests that I should put in a plug for *The Better John Guide* by Jonathan Routh (New York: G. P. Putnam's Sons, 1966) even though it only covers the possibilities in New York City. If I had gone into this subject more deeply, I would have depended a great deal on *Clean and Decent* by Lawrence Wright (New York: The Viking Press, 1960), which has as its subtitle, "The Fascinating History of the Bathroom and the Water Closet."

II. *Food and Sex*

The idea of the parallels between food and sex is obviously far from original—I have acknowledged my debt to Audrey Richards in the text—but at the time I wrote the article on which the chapter is based I was unaware of many of the antecedents. Ray Russell, at that time Executive Editor of *Playboy*, wrote me about two stories, one by Richard Matheson and one by André Maurois, in which the theme is explicit. The Matheson piece, which appeared in a collection of his science fiction stories entitled *Born of Man and Woman* (Philadelphia: Chamberlain Press, 1954), was entitled "F———." It told of a future time when food had become a four-letter word, because eating was obsolete—and when pictures of food were peddled surreptitiously as pornography.

The Maurois sketch, "An Idea for a Story," appeared in the issue of *Esquire* for July 1934, and concerned a people called the Erophagi who were nudists except for "an armlet embroidered with lovely ornaments" which covered a nipple-like growth. This growth secreted a delicious liquid which another person could absorb by suction, and which was essential to the well-being of the race. Physical love was carried out in the open; but indulgence in the nipple was entirely surreptitious. Maurois, as Russell wrote, "went right down the line, drawing all the sexual parallels, including jealousy, unrequited desire, fidelity, promiscuity."

I once made my remark, before a meeting at the World Health Organization in Geneva, about no human society dealing rationally with the food in its environment. An obviously well-traveled gentleman asked me afterward, "What about the

Chinese?" I find this hard to answer. The raw materials that go into their dishes are about the most varied of those of any cuisine. They even eat the nests of a certain species of swift (*Salangana*). It seems to me that they are prejudiced about milk, but this may not really be a prejudice—cows are not very practical animals under the conditions that prevail in much of China. It was—and remains—a thought-provoking question.

The taboo on eating dog flesh, and taboos on the eating of the meat of various other vertebrates, are discussed in a book by Frederick J. Simoons, *Eat Not This Flesh* (Madison: University of Wisconsin Press, 1961).

Since I wrote the paragraph on our attempts to buy horse meat, my wife has taken to further experimentation with animal foods. It all started from a discussion with students living on very meager resources and trying to find the cheapest meat possible. Nancy found that the canned cat food labeled "chicken parts and liver" could, with judicious seasoning, be made into a paté that everyone found delicious. She also discovered that the horse meat put up as cat food was considerably better than the dog equivalent and had possibilities, with proper seasoning. Does this mean that our taste is nearer to that of cats than of dogs?

The differing importance of hormonal (instinctive) versus learned control over sexual behavior is discussed by Frank A. Beach in his book *Hormones and Behavior* (New York: Paul Hoeber, 1948). The importance of learning in the sexual behavior of chimpanzees is brought out by R. M. Yerkes in *Chimpanzees, a Laboratory Colony* (New Haven: Yale University Press, 1943).

I have referred to Samuel Butler's *Erewhon* as though everyone is familiar with it—which I am told is not the case. First published in 1872, the book remains a cutting satire on many aspects of our civilization. As an academician, I am particularly fond of the "Colleges of Unreason." Various reprints are easily available.

III. *Three Square Meals*

The "people" advocating the Shrewsbury idea may well really be only one person, Dick Summer, of Boston's radio station WBZ. A letter to him asking for documentation got no answer—but even so he may have a case.

In checking for documentation on my comments about the mana and tabu problems of high-ranking Polynesians, I find I have almost paraphrased remarks by Douglas Oliver on page 54 of his book *The Pacific Islands* (Cambridge, Mass.: Harvard University Press, 1951), though I do not remember consulting the book while writing. Oliver's book remains the best general account of Pacific peoples.

Each time I write a book I resolve to keep careful track of my sources for secondhand material as I write. But each time I forget something important. In the present case, I simply cannot trace the information about the eleventh-century Byzantine princess with the fork, or the jeweled forks of the first Queen Elizabeth of England. I do find many notes about forks that I did not use, such as a letter read to the British Archaeological Society on 21 December 1837 and published in *Archaeologia*, vol. 25, pp. 301–305, describing a two-pronged fork closely associated with coins dating from 796–890 A.D. Thus there is apparently clear evidence that the fork existed in England in the ninth century, though hardly known until later times. In the Oxford English Dictionary the first quotation under the definition of "fork," dated 1463, is from a will bequeathing "my silvir forke for grene gyngour," and the second, also from a will, concerns a "spone with a forke in the end."

I consulted a number of textbooks on nutrition in the course of gathering material for this chapter—but mostly this experience simply reinforced my prejudice against textbooks of all kinds. I learned more from talks with a delightful lady, the late Adelia Beeuwkes, who was Professor of Public Health Nutrition here at the University of Michigan.

My favorite among books on food is *The Origin of Food Habits* by H. D. Renner (London: Faber and Faber, 1944). It is a mine of information on a wide variety of topics related to food. Vilhjalmur Stefansson described his meat-diet experience in a book, *Not by Bread Alone* (New York: Macmillan, 1946).

L. S. B. Leakey's work on Zinjanthropus and his later discoveries are discussed in all contemporary anthropology texts. He himself has written numerous articles in technical publications and one book on the subject, *The Progress and Evolu-*

tion of Man in Africa (New York: Oxford University Press, 1961). Raymond Dart wrote up his ideas about the Australopithecines in a book entitled *Adventures with the Missing Link* (New York: Harper, 1959). My figures on the animals the Australopithecines hunted come from this book.

The idea that maize and wheat were first used in parched form is developed by Paul Mangelsdorf in two articles in *Scientific American:* "The Mystery of Corn" in the July 1950 issue, and "Wheat" in the July 1953 issue. Much of our knowledge of the development of agriculture and village life in the Near East comes from excavations supervised by R. J. Braidwood and reported in numerous technical articles. His book *Prehistoric Men* (Chicago: Chicago Natural History Museum, 5th ed., 1961) includes a summary of his findings.

My reference to Robert Graves and the Greek attitude toward beans comes from his two-volume work *The Greek Myths* (Baltimore: Penguin Books, 1955), entry 98.8. There are numerous references to Greek food habits scattered through this fascinating work.

IV. *Insects in the Diet*

I think Charles Elton first used the phrase "key industry animals" for insects and other animals living directly off plants in a little book entitled *Animal Ecology* (New York: Macmillan, 1927). Elton is one of those rare scientists whose writings form a mine of apt phrases and quotable remarks.

I got the recipe for ambrosia from Robert Graves, *The Greek Myths,* cited in the notes on the previous chapter. Almost all of my other information came from F. S. Bodenheimer's *Insects as Human Food* (The Hague: W. Junk, 1951), and I hope my debt to him is obvious enough from the text. His book has an extensive bibliography and I have often gone back to his sources to check on details, but I see no point in repeating references here, since anyone interested in pursuing the subject further should start with the Bodenheimer book.

V. *Sex: Male, Female, Other*

The bizarre habits of the bowerbirds of New Guinea and Australia have gained increasing attention from students of animal behavior. A. J. Marshall wrote a book on them:

Bower-birds (Oxford: Clarendon Press, 1954). My statistics on the objects they collect come from an article by the late Thomas Gilliard, "Evolution of Bowerbirds," in the issue of *Scientific American* for August 1963.

Raymond Pearl's data on frequency of copulation and conception are from *The Natural History of Population* (New York: Oxford University Press, 1939).

The standard work on sexual physiology in animals in general (including man) is *Sex and Internal Secretions,* in two volumes, edited by William C. Young (Baltimore: Williams and Wilkins, 3rd ed., 1961). I have consulted this frequently, but failed to make notes on which ideas I got where in the course of browsing. *Human Sexual Response,* by W. H. Masters and Virginia E. Johnson, was published after my manuscript was written, but looking through it I fail to find any discussion of periodicity in female sexual desire, which in itself seems significant.

The standard cross-cultural survey of sexual customs among human societies is that by Clellan S. Ford and Frank A. Beach, *Patterns of Sexual Behavior* (New York: Harper, 1951). An excellent account of the various modern field studies of primate behavior, written by the experts most deeply involved, has been edited by Irven DeVore under the title *Primate Behavior* (New York: Holt, Rinehart and Winston, 1965). This has a detailed bibliography. The authors whom I have mentioned in the text, and whose works I have consulted most often, are:

C. R. Carpenter, "A Field Study of the Behavior and Social Relations of Howling Monkeys," in *Comparative Psychological Monographs,* vol. 10, pp. 1–168, 1934.

———, "A Field Study in Siam of the Behavior and Social Relations of the Gibbon, *Hylobates lar,*" in the same journal, vol. 16, pp. 1–212, 1940.

George Schaller, *The Mountain Gorilla: Ecology and Behavior* (Chicago: University of Chicago Press, 1963).

———, *The Year of the Gorilla* (Chicago: Univ. of Chicago Press, 1964; this written in an easy narrative style, but containing the essential observations).

Vernon Reynolds, *Budongo; An African Forest and Its*

Chimpanzees (New York: The Natural History Press, 1965).

The Reynolds quotation is from page 419 in their chapter on chimpanzees in the book edited by DeVore. Other chapters in the DeVore book provide good summaries of the studies of Sherwood Washburn, Jane Goodall and the Japanese scientists mentioned in the text.

The idea that man should be looked at as a "self-domesticated animal" is explored in some detail in a book by Weston La Barre, *The Human Animal* (Chicago: University of Chicago Press, 1954).

The influence of hormones on human sexual behavior is discussed at many points in the two volumes edited by William C. Young, cited earlier. The subject of the role of hormones in homosexuality (or rather, the absence of hormonal influence) gets especial attention in the chapter by John L. and Joan G. Hampson, "The Ontogenesis of Sexual Behavior in Man," where references to the technical literature may be found. Medical and psychological writing on homosexuality is voluminous and often confusingly contradictory. In this, as in many other aspects of sex, I have found the two volumes of *The Encyclopedia of Sexual Behavior,* edited by Albert Ellis and Albert Abarbanel (New York: Hawthorn Books, 1961), a helpful guide through the maze of conflicting opinions and observations.

vi. *Incest and Cannibalism*

For material on incest I have depended a great deal on R. E. L. Masters, *Patterns of Incest* (New York: The Julian Press, 1963). In the latter part of this book Masters has included a series of articles on particular aspects of incest written by authorities in the respective fields.

There is an article entitled "Incest in Mormonism" by Theodore Schroeder in the *American Journal of Urology and Sexology,* Vol. 11, No. 10, October 1915.

I promised, in the text, to cite some of the books in which the history of Western attitudes toward sex is discussed. Those that I remember particularly are:

Wayland Young, *Eros Denied: Sex in Western Society* (New York: Grove Press, 1964).

G. Rattray Taylor, *Sex in History* (New York: Vanguard Press, 1954).

Richard Lewinsohn, *A History of Sexual Customs* (New York: Harper, 1958).

I am in no position to judge the relative merits of these books—I don't believe any of the three had much influence on my thinking. I do however still vividly remember the effect of reading, many years ago, Edward Westermarck's *Christianity and Morals* (London: Kegan Paul, Trench, Trubner & Co., 1939). I think this first led me to realize that the Western world had no particular patent on moral atttiudes. More recently I have greatly admired and often consulted Crane Brinton's *A History of Western Morals* (New York: Harcourt, Brace, 1959), though Brinton, good historian that he is, comes up with no sweeping generalizations.

I regret to say that I cannot now find where I got the reference to incest in the code of Justinian. I've looked for Justinian in the index of a number of likely sources—with no success. The genetic consequences of incest are discussed in the authoritative book by Curt Stern, *Principles of Human Genetics* (San Francisco: W. H. Freeman, 2nd ed., 1960). The Canada goose item comes secondhand from an article by David Aberle and others, "The Incest Taboo and the Mating Patterns of Animals," in the issue of the *American Anthropologist* for April 1963 (vol. 65, pp. 253–265). This article has an extensive bibliography for original sources.

Leslie A. White's ideas about the origin of incest are developed in a chapter of *The Science of Culture* (New York: Farrar, Straus, 1949), where he makes frequent reference to the work of that pioneer anthropologist E. B. Tylor.

My account of incest among the gods and in mythology is based largely on a chapter in the book on incest by Masters. The idea that Ham committed incest with his drunken father comes from here, attributed to "some interpreters of the Scriptures" as the reason for Ham's condemnation to slavery. I have not, however, come across any very scholarly discussion of this point.

The story of the Donner episode has been told by George Stewart in a book, *Ordeal by Hunger* (Boston: Houghton Mifflin, 1936).

The special study of disgust mentioned in the text was made by Dr. A. Angyal and published under the title "Disgust and Related Aversions" in the *Journal of Abnormal and Social Psychology,* vol. 36 (1941), pp. 393–412.

VII. *On Being Mean*

My interest in the problem of finding a reasonable classification for the different varieties of behavior started when I became involved in the planning of a book which subsequently appeared under the title *Behavior and Evolution,* edited by Anne Roe and G. G. Simpson (New Haven: Yale University Press, 1958). The book includes a section on "Categories of Behavior," with an excellent chapter on territoriality by C. R. Carpenter; but aggression is hardly mentioned anywhere except in the chapter on human behavior by L. Z. Freedman and Anne Roe.

There is no mention of play in the Roe and Simpson book, which seems to me particularly surprising now because I have come to suspect that it has been especially important in the evolution of human behavior. The most complete study of play known to me is a book by Johan Huizinga, *Homo ludens,* available in a paperback edition published by Beacon Press.

Robert Ardrey has included a particularly detailed bibliography (though limited to books or articles available in English) on studies of animal aggression in *The Territorial Imperative* (New York: Atheneum, 1966). The bibliography in Konrad Lorenz's *On Aggression* (New York: Harcourt, Brace & World, 1966) includes more technical references and covers much material that is available only in German. There is nothing on the subject of aggressive behavior in animals that I could add to these two lists. All of the studies that I have consulted are included, and many more besides.

I agree with the basic thesis of both Lorenz and Ardrey that much of the animal remains in man and that social scientists have tended to neglect this heritage. I am greatly impressed, however, by the ways in which our animal background has been modified by cultural factors and I think that both authors, understandably, have oversimplified. "Aggression," I suspect, is a sort of wastebasket word in which many different aspects of human behavior have been collected.

VIII. *Shortcuts to Happiness*

In this chapter I have depended very largely on Lewis Lewin, *Phantastica, Narcotic and Stimulating Drugs* (reissued by E. P. Dutton, 1964), as I hope is obvious from the text. For a summary of more recent work I have used Robert S. de Ropp, *Drugs and the Mind* (New York: St. Martin's Press, 1957). De Ropp's attitude toward the perplexing problems of the addictive drugs appeals to me as reasonable and objective. He gives a good account of the consequences of our present treatment of marijuana, which I judge to be the product of prejudice rather than reason. David Solomon has put together a fascinating anthology on the subject, *The Marihuana Papers* (Indianapolis: Bobbs-Merrill, 1966).

I have long been interested in alcohol and have read a great deal on the subject. My immediate source has been the symposium on *Alcohol and Civilization* edited by Salvatore P. Lucia (New York: McGraw-Hill, 1963), especially chapters on "The Antiquity of Alcohol in Diet and Medicine," by Dr. Lucia himself, and "Alcohol in Human Culture," by Berton Roueché. I have also at times consulted Roueché's popular book on alcohol, *The Neutral Spirit* (Boston: Little, Brown, 1960).

There is a great deal of information in a book edited by Raymond G. McCarthy, *Drinking and Intoxication; Selected Readings in Social Attitudes and Controls* (Glencoe, Ill.: The Free Press, 1959). The last part of the book contains a series of articles on prohibition and repeal in the United States, from which I have garnered most of my facts on this phenomenon. Other books that were frequently consulted in writing are Chandler Washburne, *Primitive Drinking* (New York and New Haven: College and University Press Publishers, 1961), and Gerald Carson, *The Social History of Bourbon* (Dodd, Mead, 1963). Since this chapter was written a fascinating "ethnography of bar behavior" has been published: *Liquor License,* by Sherri Cavan (Chicago: Aldine Publishing Company, 1966).

IX. *The Pursuit of Gentility*

For information about the history of pornography, I have depended very largely on three books:

Eberhard and Phyllis Kronhausen, *Pornography and the Law* (New York: Ballantine Books, rev. ed. 1964).

H. Montgomery Hyde, *A History of Pornography* (New York: Farrar, Straus & Giroux, 1965).

Morris L. Ernst and Alan U. Schwartz, *Censorship: The Search for the Obscene* (New York: Macmillan, 1964).

Since this chapter was written, the United States Supreme Court has added more confusion than clarification to the problem of what is publishable by their decision of March 21, 1966, in the cases of Ralph Ginzburg, Edward Mishkin and *Fanny Hill*. The confusion is carefully examined by Jason Epstein in an article, "The Obscenity Business," in the *Atlantic Monthly*, August 1966.

The Anatomy of Dirty Words, by Edward Sagarin, was published in 1962 by Lyle Stuart in New York. My linguist friends view some of the discussion with raised eyebrows—but certainly the book is both amusing and instructive. I have also often consulted a *Dictionary of Medical Slang* by J. E. Schmidt (Springfield, Ill.: Charles C Thomas, 1959) though I have not used material from it in the text. Medical obscenities are often picturesque and frequently mix metaphors from food and sex. Opening the book at random I find for instance, "Jink the jam . . . Spurt the phallic ardent stream." Or, "Raw meat . . . A female, esp. a prostitute, who submits naked to the sexual act."

Readers of this chapter have commented that I have concentrated too exclusively on the absurdities of modern Western civilization—that we have no patent on gentility. I doubt whether any other civilization has introduced quite as many complications into sexual behavior as we have, but every culture has some complex system of manners to govern behavior and these at times must irk at least a few individuals. But every anthropology book touches on this, and my own experiences with non-Western peoples have not been profound enough to give me any feeling of special insight. In the matter of etiquette, I found myself fascinated by a book on tenth-century Japan by Ivan Morris, *The World of the Shining Prince* (New York: Alfred A. Knopf, 1964). The Japanese seem for long to have given special attention to the formalities of interpersonal relations; some of my Japanese friends, at least, admit that they find this an almost intolerable nuisance.

The subtleties of gesture and of spatial relations among people have been studied in detail by one anthropologist, Edward T. Hall, who has explored their implications in two books, *The Silent Language* (New York: Doubleday, 1959) and *The Hidden Dimension* (New York: Doubleday, 1966). These books should have wide interest for anyone concerned with cultural variations in the behavior of the human animal.

x. *Covering Up: What to Wear*

My main source for this chapter has obviously been J. C. Flügel, *The Psychology of Clothes* (London: The Hogarth Press, 1930), No. 18 in "The International Psycho-analytical Library." I have also found Lawrence Langner's *The Importance of Wearing Clothes* (New York: Hastings House, 1959) both thought-provoking and useful, though his main concern is with aspects of esthetics and behavior that I have been little concerned with in this chapter.

There are many books on costume, often elaborately illustrated. A standard work on the history of costume is Hilaire Hiler, *From Nudity to Raiment* (New York: The Educational Press, 1930). A recent book which I have consulted frequently but not used much because of my different approach is by Blanche Payne, *History of Costume* (New York: Harper & Row, 1965). This has a good bibliography of books on the subject. The topic of "provocation," including both modesty and advertisement is, of course, often dealt with in the literature on sexual behavior. There is, for instance, quite a deal about clothes in Richard Lewinsohn's *A History of Sexual Customs* (New York: Harper, 1958) and in various articles in *The Encyclopedia of Sexual Behavior,* cited in the notes for Chapter V.

There is also a great deal about clothes and ornament in the anthropological literature, and I am sure I have picked up many of my ideas in the course of reading in this field, though I can no longer pinpoint sources. I do know that my early thinking about the origin of clothing was influenced by the ideas of Ernest Crawley, especially as expressed in *Dress, Drinks and Drums* (London: Methuen, 1931; edited by Theodore Besterman).

I have avoided the physiological aspects of the protective

function of clothing because I dealt with that in a chapter in *Where Winter Never Comes* (New York: Scribner's, 1952) and my ideas have not changed much.

There are all sorts of fascinating byways in this topic of clothing and bodily ornamentation, and my problem in writing has been to avoid getting lost in them. I cannot resist mentioning two books that I have read, even though they were not directly used in writing the text: C. W. and Phillis Cunnington, *The History of Underclothes* (London: Michael Joseph, 1951) and Albert Parry, *Tattoo* (New York: Simon and Schuster, 1933). The latter book is not a general history of the subject, but rather deals with practices by modern natives of the United States, with all sorts of insights on the psychology of this form of ornamentation.

XI. *Subcultures and Contracultures*

Most of the books and articles used in writing this chapter have been cited in the text. I have also, as in the case of my remarks on the Mafia, depended on articles in various current encyclopedias.

Of the numerous nonfiction books on homosexuality, the one that has appealed to me as most revealing is *The Homosexual in America* by Donald Webster Cory (New York: Castle Books, rev. ed., 1960). An appendix in this book includes a list of works of fiction dealing with the subject. I find the psychoanalytical literature confusing and I have not depended on it much in writing the various parts of this book concerned with homosexuality. This clinical approach, however, is covered in a recent book by Irving Bieber and others, *Homosexuality, A Psychoanalytical Study* (New York: Basic Books, 1962), which has a good bibliography of relevant studies. The book by Benjamin and Masters on *Prostitution and Morality* cited in the text has a chapter devoted to the subject of male hustlers. An article on "The Social Integration of Queers and Peers" by Albert J. Reiss Jr. is reprinted in an anthology edited by Howard S. Becker, *The Other Side* (Glencoe, Ill.: The Free Press, 1964), which contains much other material relevant to the problems of deviance from social norms.

The academic subculture is often dealt with in fiction—understandably enough since so many of our novelists now hold professorships. The three novels on academic themes that have seemed to me particularly interesting from the point of view of understanding the subculture are:

Mary McCarthy, *The Groves of Academe* (New York: Harcourt, Brace, 1952).

Randall Jarrell, *Pictures from an Institution* (New York: Alfred A. Knopf, 1954).

Stringfellow Barr, *Purely Academic* (New York: Simon and Schuster, 1958).

When one thinks that Academia is also the habitat of historians, sociologists, psychologists and the like, it is remarkable how little attention they have paid to the environment in which they live—at least in print. One sociological study that caused a certain amount of furor among the professors because it cut through so many pretensions is *The Academic Marketplace,* by Theodore Caplow and Reece J. McGee (New York: Basic Books, 1958). I have learned a great deal about the history of Academia from *The Development of Academic Freedom in the United States,* by Richard Hofstadter and Walter P. Metzger, and *Academic Freedom in Our Time,* by Robert M. MacIver (both New York: Columbia University Press, 1955).

XII. *Crackpots, Phonies and Squares*

I have long been interested in personality theory, and have collected a considerable number of books on the subject lining a shelf facing me here in my study. I have read some of these books and thumbed through others, but without gaining much understanding, as is probably clear enough from the way I have written the text of this chapter. Certainly I have no feeling of confidence as a guide for suggesting reading to anyone else, so I shall limit myself to citing books, not mentioned in the text, that I remember as having some influence on my thinking.

The eugenics idea—which I have called genetic determinism —is most persuasively presented by Garrett Hardin in *Nature and Man's Fate* (New York: Rinehart, 1959). It seems to me that he goes much too far in attributing undesirable traits to the genes; but since experimental breeding is out of the question with people, this is necessarily a matter of opinion.

On the matter of physique and temperament, there is an extensive and partially annotated bibliography in *The Varieties of Human Physique*, by W. H. Sheldon (New York: Harper, 1940). Sheldon's own ideas about personality types are developed in a later book, *The Varieties of Temperament* (New York: Harper, 1942), a book in which he takes many pot-shots at the clinical psychologists.

Most of my information about phrenology and the like comes from encyclopedia articles. I found a rich mine of phony examples in an amusing book by Curtis D. MacDougall entitled simply *Hoaxes* (New York: Macmillan, 1940). The curious case of Piltdown man is described in a book by J. S. Weiner, *The Piltdown Forgery* (New York: Oxford University Press, 1955).

Ideas about food that could reasonably be considered "crack-pot" have been prevalent since ancient times, but seem to flourish with particular vigor in the modern United States. Ronald M. Deutsch has written an amusing book on this, entitled *The Nuts among the Berries* (New York: Ballantine Books, rev. ed., 1967).

XIII. *Priests and Policemen*

We got a considerable collection of books on police and on religion from the library in the course of writing this chapter—but we made little use of them except for the titles mentioned in the text.

XIV. *Toward Utopia*

Two books on utopias have been particularly useful in my pursuit of the subject in the course of discussions with students:

Glenn Negley and J. Max Patrick, *The Quest for Utopia; An Anthology of Imaginary Societies* (New York: Henry Schuman, 1952).

Chad Walsh, *From Utopia to Nightmare* (New York: Harper & Row, 1962).

George Gaylord Simpson has developed the idea of evolution as a relay race in his chapter on "The History of Life" in *Evolution after Darwin,* Vol. I (Chicago: University of Chicago Press, 1960).

The relevance of biological ideas to human behavior and ethics has been discussed by Simpson in *The Meaning of Evolution* (New Haven: Yale University Press, 1950); by Julian Huxley in *Touchstone for Ethics* (New York: Harper, 1947); and in most detail by C. H. Waddington in *The Ethical Animal* (New York: Atheneum, 1961).

The whole idea of the value of diversity has been explored by John R. Platt in an article entitled "Diversity" in the issue of *Science* for December 2, 1966 (Vol. 154, No. 3753, pp. 1132–39).

I end with man as a toolmaker; tools of course are really a far less important characteristic than ideas. The ways by which man may have developed these are discussed by Lewis Mumford in *The Myth of the Machine* (New York: Harcourt, Brace & World, 1967).

ABOUT THE AUTHOR

IN 1916, when he was ten years old, Marston Bates' family moved from Grand Rapids, Michigan, to a farm in Fort Lauderdale, Florida. An only child in a rather isolated environment, he became intensely interested in insects, and obsessed with the idea of going to the tropics.

Mr. Bates was graduated from the University of Florida in 1927, and went to work for the United Fruit Company in Honduras and Guatemala. He received his Ph.D. from Harvard in 1934. After working for the Rockefeller Foundation studying tropical diseases in Albania, Egypt, and Colombia, Mr. Bates transferred to the Foundation's New York office, where—as Special Assistant to the President—he explored the relations between public health and human population problems. He resigned in 1952 to become Professor of Zoology at the University of Michigan.

Mr. Bates is the author of, among other books, the *Nature of Natural History, The Forest and the Sea* and *Man in Nature*. He also writes a monthly column for *Natural History* magazine.

The Bates family includes four children. Mrs. Bates, the former Nancy Bell Fairchild, is the author of *East of the Andes and West of Nowhere*.